O B J E C T

A book series about the hidden lives of ordinary things.

Series Editors:

Ian Bogost and Christopher Schaberg

Advisory Board:

Sara Ahmed, Jane Bennett, Johanna Drucker, Raiford Guins, Graham Harman, renée hoogland, Pam Houston, Eileen Joy, Douglas Kahn, Daniel Miller, Esther Milne, Timothy Morton, Nigel Thrift, Kathleen Stewart, Rob Walker, Michele White.

In association with

LOYOLA UNIVERSITY NEW ORLEANS · Georgia Tech | Center for Media Studies

BOOKS IN THE SERIES

drone

ADAM ROTHSTEIN

Bloomsbury Academic
An imprint of Bloomsbury Publishing Inc

B L O O M S B U R Y
NEW YORK · LONDON · NEW DELHI · SYDNEY

Bloomsbury Academic
An imprint of Bloomsbury Publishing Inc

1385 Broadway	50 Bedford Square
New York	London
NY 10018	WC1B 3DP
USA	UK

www.bloomsbury.com

**BLOOMSBURY and the Diana logo are trademarks
of Bloomsbury Publishing Plc**

First published 2015

© Adam Rothstein, 2015

Library of Congress Cataloging-in-Publication Data
Rothstein, Adam.
Drone/by Adam Rothstein. – First edition.
pages cm. – (Object lessons)
Includes bibliographical references and index.
ISBN 978-1-62892-768-9 (hardback: alk. paper) – ISBN 978-1-62892-632-3
(pbk.: alk. paper) 1. Drone aircraft. I. Title.
UG1242.D7R68 2015
629.133'3–dc23
2014029892

ISBN: PB: 978-1-6289-2632-3
ePDF: 978-1-6289-2967-6
ePub: 978-1-6289-2525-8

Series: Object Lessons

Typeset by Deanta Global Publishing Services, Chennai, India
Printed and bound in the United States of America

To M—for always helping,
even when she doesn't think she is.

CONTENTS

INTRODUCTION

We know what a drone is. But at the same time, we don't.

Chris Anderson, CEO of drone manufacturer 3D Robotics, has said that today's drone companies are similar to the early personal computer companies of the 1970s and 1980s. Edwin Teller, inventor of the hydrogen bomb, said in 1981 that unpiloted aerial vehicles were as important as computers in the 1930s. Computer companies in the 1970s wanted to build the "Model T" of personal computers. Do these narratives conflict, or do they cohere?

We have heard about the drone, but we have heard different and contradictory things. Whether one is for them, against them, or neither, the overwhelming cacophony means this technology is significant, whether its potential is for progress or for cataclysm. It is a heavy object, full of undiagnosed complications.

The drone is cutting-edge technology, but traces its evolution back over 100 years. The drone exists, taking to the skies above our heads every day. But it also doesn't exist, because it is shrouded in fantasy. The reality of the technology includes not only fact and fiction, but also hope and fear, our complicated history, and our plans for the future. The drone, separated from and connected to the truth, has become a composite caricature of technology. It is based upon truth, but spun from a swarm of diverging narratives. These narratives tell as much about us and how we interact with technology in general, as about the drone itself.

These high-profile analogies are *definitional* narratives that attempt to explain what the technology is, and what the technology isn't. They attempt to draw a boundary line between this technology and other technologies. When we attempt to understand a new class of technology, we use this sort of analogy to symbolize the role we want this technology to play. But as it turns out, new technologies are mostly evolutions of previous technology. The drone is a means of a basic transportation revolution not unlike the car. The drone is an aircraft, it is a computer, and it is also a robot.

But even the definitions of these older technologies are complex. We have *invention* narratives that tell us the Wright Brothers invented the airplane, that Henry Ford invented the Model T, and that IBM invented the personal computer. Yet these narratives forget the Wright Brothers' wind tunnel, the importance of plate-glass and paint technology to the car, who really wrote the MS-DOS software, and countless other important intersections. The drone has its own forgotten stories as well.

We need to learn the *historical* narratives of what this technology was in the past, though it may be different now.

Did you know the first time a drone hit a target with a missile was in 1971? But video technology then was not good enough to spot targets live in the field. Still, the 1960s and 1970s saw much success for drones taking photos with analog cameras, and elements of their design have found their way to today's drones. But contemporary drones are a digital technology, and wholly different. Or are they?

We have *contemporary* narratives, evolved from that history, of what we think this technology means now. We think that drone agricultural monitors, industrial-welding robots, and drone police surveillance exist because these jobs fall into the "Three D's": they are dull, dirty, or dangerous. But this is largely a myth, perpetuated by the roots of the "robot" in a fictional narrative of human-made machines taking over serf labor. In fact, it is the jobs given to robots for reasons of economy and engineering that often become dull, dirty, and dangerous when the automated machine is tailored to a specific task. These tasks need not be single-serving jobs, but we have designed them to be, to take economic advantage of available technology.

But fictional ideas are important to how we interact with technology. *Speculative* narratives, constructed in our present, guide development for the future. Science fiction has a peculiar relationship to reality, and by focusing on our fantasies and nightmares, we may bypass a better future that technology could offer, or ignore the ill effects we are perpetuating today. If all we can imagine is delivering missiles or Amazon packages with drones, that is all the technology will do or fail to do, regardless of what tasks the technology may be best suited to accomplish. Imagining the worst-case dystopian solution is not necessarily a way out—we have to imagine the future we want to have.

We call these *intentional* narratives. We use them to justify our actions and guide development in the present. If we think we are designing a drone to deliver humanitarian aid rather than weapons, like those drones proposed by the start-up Matternet, this guides our actions via a different ethical justification. But many things can happen when a drone takes to the air, not all of which we intend. We may think a drone is not weaponized, until its collected data justifies the use of weapons. We may not think a drone poses a hazard to other aircraft, until we discover a failure scenario we didn't predict. We'll be forced to deal with those consequences even if we don't intend for them to happen. Even the most optimistically rendered Photoshop image of a drone delivering medical supplies can't change the reality of what happens when that drone loses its radio link.

Our intentions and other narratives aren't just formed individually, but often collaboratively, networked in a web of other *social* narratives. And at the same time as we collaborate on describing our visions and our fears, we still talk past each other in competing narratives. When an anti-war protester, a congressperson, and a drone hobbyist talk about drones, they are talking about entirely different things. How do we hear what each of these parties has to say, and how do we form our own thoughts from their words, so that we can better understand the landscape of plans and concerns?

The drone changes *esthetic* narratives as well. The way that the bulbous radome of a military drone looks, the way the video coming from its camera builds a view point of war, the way the sound of the drone's propeller buzzing constantly overhead sounds, and the way that the interfaces for military and civilian drones make us think—all effect our outlook on the world. For years, the best way to drive a vehicle was with an egocentric perspective—as if the car or plane was us. Similarly, we think about computers and industrial equipment as something outside us, which we look into, control with an interface, and guide around us. But drones change these traditions. Sometimes drone control is easier if we think about it as something that we look at, not something we're inside of. And in order to understand semi-autonomous automated systems, a certain amount of anthropomorphization of machines is, perhaps, necessary. And yet, as of 2004, 50 percent of military drone accidents were attributable to human factors, so whatever the best interface between humans and automated technology is, we are still developing it.

These many different drone stories are *expressive* narratives. The power of a drone to kill can be monstrous. The viewpoint from a drone's camera flying over us can be awe-inspiring. The way that swarm behavior allows a group of drones to seamlessly navigate through a small space can be amazing, intelligent, or even creepy. These feelings are parts of narratives about ourselves, but told through our technology. When we empathize with a cute-looking robot or fear the cold, expressionless head of a military drone's radome, we are really interacting with our own selves and culture, in technological form.

And this is why the drone is so important, and why we know it well, even though we are entirely confused by it. The drone is a collection of different narratives, but these narratives are the way that we work with, think about, and respond to technology. Regardless of what the future is for drones, we will continue to develop new technology. And we will continue to deal with narratives of that technology, in all their convoluted and twisted pathways.

The drone is a time traveler, spanning years of history: from the first flight of the Wright Brothers in 1903, to the first spy satellites that transmitted digital images in 1976, to the rollout of the Federal Aviation Administration's NextGen air-traffic control system, due to take effect in 2020. The drone is a shape-shifter, changing its appearance depending on place and time and what we are using it to do: it's been a target for training pilots, it's been a top-secret stealth spy vehicle, and it's been a smartphone toy. The drone is a trickster, playing upon our preconceptions and emotions, in order to manipulate our thinking even as we control it by remote. Headlines tell of "zombie drones," plans for drone terrorist attacks, and "government drone-hunting licenses" being proposed.

The drone is a monster, capable of terrible acts; and it is a hero, uniting disparate technological forces into a power greater than the sum of its parts. We must unravel these stories one by one, untangling them and reassembling them into our narrative of the drone. This is but a slim volume, but it will attempt to be a guide for making sense of these technological narratives. This book will not commit to one narrative over the others, but seek to engage with all of them, in their places. We start with the drone as it exists today, but we must not end our work here. As technology evolves, the untangling of narrative must continue—with the drone and also with any technology that finds itself in such an important position in our society.

If the story of drone technology is a story about us, it is about time we opened that book.

1 FOUR TECHNOLOGY STORIES

To set the stage for our examination of the drone's narratives, we are first going to look at four other technological narratives, which might be more familiar: the automobile, the aircraft, the computer, and the robot. The drone is very similar to these four technologies. It is a transportation paradigm shift, it is a flying machine, it is composed of computational electronics, and it is an automated robot. But nothing in history is a simple analogy. All technologies develop in fits and starts, change drastically during their development, and rely upon the development of related technologies in various ways. An analogy between two technologies may be apt in one sense, but a tremendous distortion of the facts from a different point of view. As we use these four narratives to explore drone technology, we'll see which comparisons are useful and which are not, and how history can be reduced to a single story only carefully, through conscientious design.

The automobile

The automobile industry grew into a huge economic force by linking a number of important technological and economic advances into a single product, though not in a singular instance. In the United States that product was driven by a clear societal need—reliable personal transportation in both urban and rural settings. Fulfilling this need converted the automobile from simply a useful technological device into a full-fledged culture.

Depending on the definition one uses, the automobile was invented sometime between 1860 and 1891, either in the United States, France, or Germany. The first car running on gasoline was built by Etienne Lenoir in 1860, and included a spark plug and battery. The first 4-stroke engine was built by Nicholaus Otto in 1876, even though it wasn't originally his idea. Gottlieb Daimler's 1885 engine became the prototype for modern engines, with carburetor- and cam-operated valves, and allowed the 1901 Mercedes to be the first "proper car."[1] But it was the Systeme Panhard, originating in France in 1891, that put the engine in the front of the car with a crankshaft parallel to the longitudinal axis rather than the axles, which allowed for bigger engines and solidified the assemblage's transition from "horseless carriage" to car.[2]

The vagueness of the car concept gave it a limited existence as intellectual property. In the United States, a man named George B. Selden was awarded the patent for the automobile

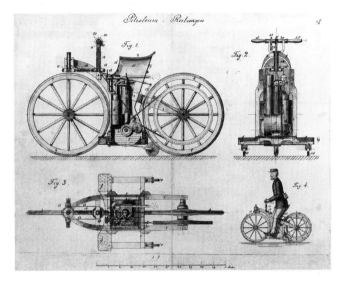

FIGURE 1 Daimler Reitwagen. More motorcycle than car, the 1885 Daimler Reitwagen was the first vehicle to use Daimler's internal combustion engine. Image in the public domain, sourced from Wikipedia.

on the basis of theorizing the concept in 1879, although he only built an engine, never an actual vehicle. In England, Harry J. Lawson attempted a monopoly by buying up the rights to various foreign patents for essential components, but was rebuked. British courts viewed the evolution of automotive technology as too rapid and disparate to be patented outright—owning the rights to any specific engine type simply caused others to slightly alter their components to avoid the law. Meanwhile, back in the United States, Selden's patent was held in trust by the Association of Licensed Automobile Manufacturers, which attempted to create a quasi-monopoly by preventing smaller manufacturers from obtaining a license.[3] While the legal action of the ALAM did have an effect of reducing the number and range of competitive car models in early years, it drew powerful opposition from Ford and other independent manufacturers. The ALAM lost an important court battle in 1909 that limited their licensing abilities, only to have Selden's patent expire in 1912.[4] After this brief stall, automotive technology in the United States boomed, generating over 1,900 car companies producing 3,000 separate makes of automobile in the 85 years after Charles Duryea sold his original vehicle on the continent.[5] Which of these 3,000 makes is the single, definitional example of a car? All of them—and none. The real import of the car would be not any particular car, but the vast number of them together, spread out across the world, drastically changing society.

When the car was first invented, it was a far cry from a transportation mainstay. It was a toy for wealthy individuals, who didn't mind contracting with blacksmiths or getting greasy themselves to do frequent maintenance and repairs. Until Charles Kettering invented the electric starter in 1911, starting a car by crank could break a person's arm if done incorrectly. It was a tinkering project and a curiosity, a technological oddity for use by "wealthy sportsmen"—perhaps an analog of "makers" today.[6] But the furious pace of innovation evolved automobiles into reliable, indispensable transportation tools. Headlights, vulcanized rubber, batteries, new paint, steel, and plate glass were all crucial developments in defining the car. As technology improved it was standardized, making mass production possible at scales entirely new to history. Critics, who derided the machines as a fad, as dangerous, or a luxury for the rich, soon found themselves complaining about the lack of parking and police speed traps.[7] The car would reshape not only transportation but also urban design and the basic principles of manufacturing. Unprecedented quantities of manufactured consumer goods were desired by an increasingly mobile retail society. The purchasing force now known as the middle class was born via new consumer credit, created initially to allow working families to afford their own vehicles. Over half of American families would have a car by 1927, and it would not be long before the suggestion that the United States was a "car culture" would not be a speculation, but a commonly held fact.[8]

The aircraft

The technological starting point of the aircraft was a laboratory experiment, and then a functional prototype. But the economic basis for developing aircraft technology would come not from the middle class, rather, from the military. Without its military uses, contemporary aircraft technology as we know it would not exist. And without aircraft technology, United States' domination of military research and development in the twentieth century would never have occurred as it did.

Humans fantasized about flight long before they dreamed of riding the open roads in a car, but it wasn't until the early twentieth century that we had any success at fulfilling this dream. While there were plenty of experimenters and daredevils in the 1800s, it took a pair of avid tinkerers to actually solve the physical problem of flight. Wilbur and Orville Wright differed from their peers in their successful aeronautical experiments. They collected data first, then applied it in design. Rather than simply building and crashing gliders, the brothers built a wind tunnel in their bicycle workshop and discovered properties of air flow and a lift coefficient chart that allowed them to design a successful aircraft with control in three axes—the aeronautics principle that was arguably their real invention.[9] From this work, building a functional prototype to prove the concept was almost mere ritual.

The Wright Brothers' Flyer is an inspirational symbol and proof-of-concept, but to the brothers themselves, it was always a product to be sold to the military.[10] They succeeded in selling their Flyer to the War Department, and while they made small improvements to their design and sold a number to wealthy hobbyists, the Flyer was surpassed by other designs by 1910, and the military began shopping in a growing market.[11]

Patent disputes took their toll upon this nascent industry as well. The Wrights and their main competitor Glenn Curtiss both guarded their creations litigiously, and the entire industry would orbit these two poles for the first ten years.[12] While the courts did recognize their design achievements as unique, intellectual property stood in the way of independent innovation. And with a World War on their hands, the War Department had larger problems than honoring proprietary designs. The American military wholeheartedly leapt at the prospect of building up an air force in World War One, but failed miserably. They sought mass production, but manufacturing aircraft in the manner of cars wasn't possible—the tolerances of aircraft designs were too small, and the fabric and wood material was not conducive to stamping and casting. Furthermore, the technology itself was shifting too rapidly. By the time a design was frozen for production and the products reached the front lines, the design was likely obsolete.[13] Shortages of necessary material compounded problems, and by the time any number of aircraft reached Europe the war was over, and most of the aircraft weren't worth the trouble of shipping back to the States. Mass production of aircraft would not truly be possible until full-metal aircraft became standard in the 1930s, a full thirty years into the history of aviation. Given all of these implicit challenges, the Wrights and Curtiss's full control over the aircraft market were numbered.

While there were a number of independent aircraft innovations in accessories—such as the oxygen mask, the parachute, electrically heated clothing, and the wireless—an aircraft market moving at the pace of free market economics could not evolve technology quickly enough to keep the military supplied with superior aircraft.[14] In the aftermath of the World War One debacle, Congress and the military began to tightly control the process of approving military contracts for aircraft, which would set the procedural standard for the way aircraft were researched, developed, and produced. Civil aviation never lived up to its expectations, and could not fund technological development. Mail service, crop dusting, aerial photography and survey, air patrol, and passenger service were simply not robust markets.[15] Development dollars would come from the military, and aviation companies had to submit to the procedures dictated by the military to get a piece of that pie. Civil aviation businesses only stayed open through dedication to their product or by being subsidiaries of military aircraft companies. It was this pattern of aircraft development that would become the "Total Package Procurement" model of US defense purchasing. The entire project—from research, to prototype, to production run— would be contracted out to a single company, approved at the beginning by top military officials.[16] This provided funding for applied research and guaranteed a production run for an eventual product, as long as the company worked on a project that the military had pre-approved. Therefore, a small number of companies who adapted themselves to this process became the core of the aerospace industry, the high-tech symbiotes of the US military.[17] What we now call the "military-industrial complex" emerged via this system of coordinating and funding the aeronautics industries.

While military aircraft are indeed remarkable technology, there is still a distinct separation between the old dream of flight and the contemporary reality of military air superiority.[18] Supersonic jets, spy satellites, and self-guiding munitions are all realities, but the dream of personal aircraft in every garage remains unfulfilled speculation.[19]

The computer

The computer was not a dream or a hobby, but the answer to a very specific military need. For much of its history, cutting-edge computing technology was funded by the military, but in fulfilling this need so well, certain businesses saw additional commercial opportunity. It was this commercial marketing and the following design standardization that would make the computer into a ubiquitous personal device, rather than just another state-of-the-art military technology project.

Counting devices, tabulating machines, and other calculating aids have all had their influence in computer theory, but it was Charles Babbage's nineteenth-century theoretical analytical engine that first introduced the concept of stored-data programs.[20] Merging this idea with electronics was simply a matter of time. The Electronic Numerical Integrator And Computer, or ENIAC, a computer built by John Mauchly and Presper Eckert at the University of

Pennsylvania during World War Two, was conceived as a military tool for creating ballistic tables. Previously, this important task required large numbers of people working for weeks to do the large number of complex calculations by hand.[21] The ENIAC could not store programs, and had to be rewired for each new task. Electronic calculating machines met Babbage's theory in The Manchester Baby, the first stored-program digital computer, which came out of wartime electrical calculating projects in England. Simultaneously in the Soviet Union, the MESM computer would be used for calculations to make their hydrogen bomb.[22] The purpose of these computers was first and foremost for saving time spent on routine, complex mathematics, not necessarily for inventing a new class of electronic device. Military budgets built them quickly, if engineered haphazardly. The US Department of Defense would remain the single largest procurer of software in the country through the 1970s. The phrase "software engineering" was even invented by the North Atlantic Treaty Organization to address problems in computer development that were negatively impacting strategic goals.[23]

Cars and aircraft immediately stimulated the public imagination, but the civilian world wasn't quite sure what to do with a computer. Their use was limited to those with a lot of mathematics on their plate, and nonmilitary sources of funding came from the likes of the National Bureau of Standards, as in the case of Mauchly and Eckert's successor to their pioneering ENIAC, the UNIVAC (Universal Automatic

FIGURE 2 UNIVAC on CBS. Presper Eckert and programmer Harold Sweeney show off the UNIVAC to Walter Cronkite, during the computer's 1952 appearance on CBS to correctly predict the presidential election. Image produced by the US Census Bureau, in the public domain, sourced from Haverford University.

Computer).[24] Given that this machine was designed for unglamorous tasks like processing census records, when office equipment company Remington Rand acquired the UNIVAC brand, they weren't sure how to sell it. They used the media-friendly name to sell the Remington Rand 409, marketed to businesses simply as an upgraded punch card tabulator, good for payrolls and tax returns.[25] The LEO machine in England did innovative stock tabulating work for the J. Lyons Company, as well as for Ford, Kodak, and British Railways.[26] But it wasn't until IBM started selling computers that they became a business standard.

Remington Rand launched its UNIVAC line first, but IBM's existing market domination in noncomputing office machinery won the sales battle. Other companies attempted to flood the market with a wide variety of computers, each with slight differences. IBM focused on its known commercial customer bases, designing products tailored directly for each.[27] Connecting the technology to known-use cases worked well, and IBM's computer sales monopoly became so large it quashed competing innovation, until anti-trust suits were brought against the company by the United States government in 1969.[28]

IBM would overturn its reputation as hegemonic "Big Blue" and reclaim its position as computing innovator in the personal computer evolution in the 1980s. The basic design for computers through the 1970s was time-sharing terminals linked to room-sized mainframes, but miniaturization of transistors into integrated circuits made smaller computers, or "minicomputers," a possibility. In the late 1970s, Apple and Atari both launched personal computers, marketing these new products for the wider population.[29] Models from Apple, Atari, and Tandy were popular with consumers, as were home computer kits. At first, IBM did not relish entering a market so far from business customers—its primary direction since the company was created in 1911.[30] The culture of IBM was not focused on technical innovation, but sales. Company executive Bill Lowe had to launch a secretive "independent business unit" development program in order to break out of this rut and invent a completely new type of product segment.[31] The result was the IBM PC, a new standard architecture for personal computers, with the era-defining operating system MS-DOS. The IBM PC was bigger than it had to be, to make the architecture easier for the home user to understand, access, and modify with additional components, opening it up to new uses and a wide range of compatible peripherals.[32] Retailers, peripheral makers, and consumers loved the idea. In 1982 the IBM PC was pronounced *Time* magazine's "Machine of the Year," and the standard component layout is still found in computers today.

Even the lowest-grade cell phones today have greater processing capacity than the 1982 IBM PC. Computer technology has advanced at an astounding rate, becoming so cheap and small that even devices like refrigerators, cars, and wristwatches now have computers inside them, allowing the many complicated features we now expect. From a very specific-use case, computer marketing has expanded to include anything and everything.

The robot

The automaton has always been more of a fantasy than an actual technology. However, at a certain point in history, technological development allowed a breakthrough in repeatable, mechanical precision through automation technology. This has not quite fulfilled the fantasy, but has gotten us close enough to begin seriously thinking about how we might share our world with robots.

Visions of automata go back to mythology, and are found in the words of Aristotle, Leonardo da Vinci, Daniel Defoe, and Samuel Butler. The word "robot" was coined by Karl Čapek in his 1921 play, *R.U.R.* The Czech word "robota," from which it is adopted, means serf labor, or drudgery.[33] A common trait among all automata in fiction, both recent and ancient, is that they are most often created by wizards, gods, or other geniuses with amazing powers.[34] The ability to make a machine act of its own accord is, in the human mind, on a par with the abilities of a god.

As for robots in reality, it is often said that their purpose is to do the "Three D's": jobs that are dangerous, dull, or dirty.[35] But this is largely a myth of confirmation bias, in which we find danger, dullness, and dirt in any task that a robot can be designed to do. More importantly, robotic tasks are precision work: automated tasks humans are not capable of doing for long periods of time without failure of accuracy or economy. This is the wizardry that automation technology can achieve, and the rationale for its use. The first industrial robot, Unimate, worked in a General Motors plant in 1961, welding steel with greater speed and accuracy than human workers could do at such pace. Unimate succeeded because automated welding was more precise and efficient, not because human welding was any more dangerous, dull, or dirty than other jobs. Similarly, robots that work in health care, in warehouses, defusing bombs, or even vacuuming rugs, do so not just because a human would prefer not to, but because the robot can do it quicker, better, or cheaper than the alternative. It is in cases of precision, endurance, and efficiency where the economics of automation excels.

A robot is a broad category of machine. Alan Winfield offers three definitions of a robot: "1. an artificial device that can sense its environment and purposefully act on or in that

FIGURE 3 Welding robots. These contemporary welding robots were manufactured by KUKA, and are working in a German BMW factory. This image is by BMW Werk Lepzig, and is licensed Creative Commons, sourced through Wikimedia Commons.

environment; 2. an embodied artificial intelligence; or 3. a machine that can autonomously carry out useful work."[36] New machines that fall into these categories appear every day, even if they are not as exciting or impressive as a self-driving car or a military drone. As sensors and microprocessors get cheaper and smaller, there are fewer and fewer technologies that cannot gain precision, endurance, and efficiency with the addition of automation fitting any of these three categories.

Despite the increasing ability to beneficially automate technology, we are not much closer to the deified ability of making machines that act as humans do. And even the most advanced artificial intelligences are only as powerful as the machines that they can control. All-knowing brazen heads, superhuman Frankenstein monsters, and rebellious serf machines are still firmly in the terrain of science fiction and fantasy. And yet, the spread of computing and automation technology means that robots, in the sense of Winfield's three-part definition, are quickly becoming ubiquitous.

There are elements of the drone narrative within these historical narratives. The drone has all of these technologies within it, and is similar to all of them. These four narratives are an instructive primer, and we'll refer back to them while investigating the drone. But we have quickly reviewed these narratives, and should be wary of simplifying them. We want simple stories of how the car, the aircraft, the computer, and the robot were invented. We want to succinctly affirm our understanding of what they are. But the ways that these narratives are not as simple as we wish will be what proves most interesting about them. As we dig into the drone's own historical narrative, it will be the complicated relationship between all these narratives that refuses to be simplified, where we—the most interesting historical mechanisms—will be found.

2 THE MILITARY DRONE

The circumstances of the drone's development dictate that we start with a military narrative. The drone narrative is deeply tied to a narrative of military technology—it was developed for military purposes, just as the aircraft and computer narratives were. First, we'll look at what the narrative of military technology is and why it is unique, and then we'll lay out the narrative of drones as a military technology.

Revolutions in military history

One possible way to read a historical narrative of military technology is to divide the past into particular epochs. Max Boot, in his book *War Made New*, identifies four major technologically revolutionary periods in military history: the gunpowder revolution, the first industrial revolution, the second industrial revolution, and the information revolution.[1] Boot is wary of the deterministic implications of this way of thinking, because to emphasize any one particular technology is to ignore other important factors. History is not born in a single invention; it develops over time in the interplay of social, economic, and strategic changes. Boot identifies these four periods because they are symbolic developments of a longer flow of change.

In our narrative of military technology, we will isolate a number of developments as well. These developments are not singular. They do not describe particular moments in history, when all things were universally as we describe them today. They are points at which we can see elements of the evolving process, that contribute to our current understanding of where we are and how we got here. Drones are a new technology, but we can trace relevant aspects of what they are now through these developments in the past.

Our narrative has six key developments. Where Boot begins is where we shall begin: around 1500 AD, when increased trade and complex market forces in Europe began providing a serious incentive to independent weapons developers.[2] Because territorial power centers would buy their weapons from whomever provided the best quality, regardless of location, inventing superior arms became a business opportunity more than an expression of loyalty to one's ruler. Increased profit meant more investment, which meant more invention. This market was unique to Europe. In Asia, for example, military development was conducted under the control of centralized leadership, rather than by free entities that could profit by it. This heightened arms innovation gave Europe the upper hand in particular venues (such as sea battles), but it led to instability via a constant arms race. Our first development is this *liberalized weapons market, in which every ruler was reliant upon a budget to maintain power, and constantly at the whim of new developments that could crush a previous advantage.*[3] This free market was powerful, but it could not last.

By the nineteenth century, Europe had become a delicate balance of national powers ebbing and flowing in tides of capital and new tactics, armies clashing regularly in the eddies.[4] In North America, more than one revolution was brewing. The separation of the American colonies from England had caused a serious economic setback to the British, but despite the new nation's wealth of raw materials, the United States had not yet built up manufacturing strength. Almost every weapon that was used to win the American Revolution was captured, borrowed, or bought.[5] The struggle to procure armaments had not improved much by the War of 1812, after which the American government made attempts to rectify the situation with improved estimating and accounting practices, a new naval foundry, and a naval college.[6] What would really change military development for the United States were the two national armories at Harpers Ferry and Springfield. There, the first fully interchangeable firearms in the world were built, and Eli Whitney and Samuel Colt launched what would become known as the "American System," in which standardization of parts and manufacturing processes allowed armories to evolve from a piece-by-piece custom weapons shop, to a factory capable of mass production.[7] There was an "open-door policy" at the armories, similar to the open-source concept today, in which contractors were required to share designs and techniques with each other and the government in order to win weapons contracts.[8] It had the effect of reducing the number of patents on weapons, but also increasing innovation through standardization. This was the beginning of the unique arrangements between arms developers and the US government. This is our second development, in which *open and standardized systems improved manufacturing performance, and we see a new coordination between the military and industry*. The idealized free market begins to show its cracks, as cooperation and standardization replace constant, independent competition.

Changes in manufacturing processes developed by the armories would soon spread to other industries; the production of pocket watches, sewing machines, hand tools, and more, benefited by the American System.[9] By 1855, it was being copied in Europe.[10] Additional coordination and standardization in the form of conscription, railroads, the telegraph, and the formation of the "general staff" in the military, completely changed the form of armed forces.[11] The American Civil War, in which hundreds of thousands of troops slaughtered each other over the course of five years, was proof that the American military had evolved in terribly effective ways. But the expense of developing such slaughter was increasing to a level that only nations could manage. Back in England, an 1884 naval scare prompted a new fusing of industry and military. The cost of weapons development had become so great that individual businesses couldn't single-handedly fund innovation any longer. This is our third development: *rather than business offering new inventions to the military, it would be the military that would dictate the changes to be made with large sums of appropriations funding, which industry would compete for a chance to provide.*[12]

This development establishes the pattern for aircraft manufacturing in the United States after World War One, as military funding swung power back to the government, away from the arms manufacturers. Furthermore, after the war, public disgust with all arms manufacturers was at an all-time high. This industry was considered an international trust, driving up the costs of weapons and pushing the world toward the death and destruction that necessitated their development.[13] But close relationships between the military and industry were necessary to make weapons development feasible. Components had to be supplied, designs had to be developed, tested, and modified after field trials—an extraordinarily expensive and demanding process. It was only through large expenditures on aircraft development that the United States was able to maintain a military aircraft industry, largely concentrated within two companies at the time—and it was only by exporting military aircraft to other countries that this industry would even approach profit.[14] To limit public animosity, the government would provide as much oversight and strategic guidance to defense industries as funding. In our fourth development, governments like the United States draw weapons companies closer, regulating them for both strategic good and public relations. *The relationship between the state and industry gained a just and patriotic mission, making military oversight of industry a strategic national issue for both the US and its allies.* Arms industries begin relying on the state not just for funding but for safeguarding their existence.

Keeping these pet industries' doors open was a challenge. Just before World War Two, the US aircraft industry's capacity was only half utilized, because of the great expense of keeping the air force stocked with only the most cutting-edge technology.[15] It was financially difficult to continue developing new aircraft without building large numbers of them. And it was strategically worthless to build large numbers of aircraft without keeping them on the cutting edge, technologically. Our fifth notable development is the onset of this balancing act of high tech and high industry. *The US government would not only provide financial oversight and accountability to arms manufacturers, but they would look to guide the entire distribution of the infrastructural network that allowed wars to be fought successfully.* Here, we see the roots of the military-industrial complex growing.

A new war was approaching, which would change the shape of things yet again. Throughout World War Two, the Allied and Axis powers traded technological advantages almost weekly. In the submarine warfare in the Atlantic, radar, torpex explosives, magnetic anomaly detectors, the precursors to LORAN radio beacons, the breaking of the Enigma code, discoveries in radar wavelengths, new escort-sized carriers, sonobuoys, and radio-direction finding equipment were only some of the successful technological modifications introduced in the heat of battle, each shifting the field.[16] Large wartime budgets allowed sustained, simultaneous development and production, and showed the importance of even a slight technological advance. After the war was over and commodity manufacturers had shifted back to consumer goods, specific defense-industry companies would continue to pursue this pace of development, by maintaining this development structure to meet the threat of the Soviet Union. A new scheme called "projectizing" allowed the military to grant a large sum of money to a defense company for an entire project from research, to prototyping, to production—the roots of modern "Total Package Procurement." Projectizing built the atomic bomb, and this approach was instituted into new military research hubs like the RAND Corporation and the Department of Defense Research and Engineering's Advanced Research Projects Agency. In our sixth development, *the development of projectized Total Package Procurement gave industry the freedom to develop cutting-edge military technology and its industrial capacity simultaneously, backed by the large sums of money available in the defense budget, while maintaining the military's strategic control over the direction the work would take.* It is here, in the second half of the twentieth century, where the drone would emerge as one of these projectized developments.

The historical context of the drone is rooted in these developments. When the drone was created: there was not a free market of military technology; military technology was owned and controlled by the military itself; funding was only released to companies willing to pursue what the military decided; this funding drew companies permanently under the control of the military; this control extended not just over research aims but over the fundamental infrastructure of industry itself; and within this military-industrial complex, only particular, fully conceived projects were approved and attempted. This is the sort of technology that drones are— not a civilian technology pressed into military service, but a projectized, military-funded and controlled technology, built by military-funded and controlled industry. Drones did not develop across Midwestern and European workshops, in the wind tunnel of a bicycle manufacturing company, in a Silicon Valley start-up, or in the special project division of an international corporation. Drones developed in the American military-industrial complex, and what they look like, how they work, and how they have been used all stem directly from that history.

Aircraft without pilots

The first attempts at remote-controlled aircraft occurred relatively early in the history of flight, but did not fulfill military needs well enough to stick around. Curtiss-Sperry designed an aerial torpedo in 1917. Charles Kettering—who also invented the electric starter for the car and sold business machines at National Cash Register with Thomas Watson of IBM fame—developed a radioplane in the 1910s as well.[17] These early drone-like aircraft were fused from separate cutting-edge technologies to make workable prototypes. But while the technology functioned, it did not function well enough. Only with serious strategic value would drones be developed as a technology in its own right.

The name "drone" stems from the use of target drones in the 1930s, named for their unsophisticated, noisy, insect-like flight capacities; over 15,000 remote-controlled target drones were built by the Radioplane Company during World War Two. In an interesting historical coincidence, a woman named Norma Jeane Dougherty—who would later be known as Marilyn Monroe—would be discovered by a *Stars and Stripes* photographer as she assembled a Radioplane model RP-5 in the company's Los Angeles plant.[18] While Monroe would become an international name, her drones and their cousins remained of minor influence. During the war, guided bombs of various sorts were devised, but without much strategic success.[19] Even the Germans' groundbreaking ballistic missile, the V2, would kill more concentration camp slave laborers during its construction than it ever killed with its warheads.[20]

Ryan Aeronautics, a civil aviation company drafted into World War Two production, found more success in novel military airframe design than they did in civilian aircraft sales.

Ryan first put a jet engine on a remote-controlled airframe in 1948. It was a target drone, recoverable by parachute if the training pilot failed to shoot it down.[21] Training remained a useful end, but reconnaissance was to be the drone's talent, once technology made it possible.

The idea of modifying a target drone to carry cameras was first suggested publicly in a Ryan press release in 1955, the same year that the Lockheed U-2 made its first flight. The U-2 was a secret plane designed to fly at high altitudes over the range of the Soviet Union's best surface-to-air missiles, to take photos of strategic targets below. But when Francis Gary Powers's U-2 was shot down over the Soviet Union in 1960, the military suddenly needed even better technology to avoid such embarrassment. A supersonic spy plane project was one option, designed to fly faster than the missiles.[22] Spy satellites were another option, already in development, but not yet successful. In 1962, the year that Marilyn Monroe died, the Air Force decided to pursue one more option, by signing a contract with Ryan to modify existing jet-powered Firebee drones into use for reconnaissance.[23]

Extensions of the original projectized program would evolve nearly thirty varieties of the "Lightning Bug" drone, which could do photographic reconnaissance, serve as a target drone or decoy, conduct electromagnetic warfare and surveillance, and was even rigged and tested to deploy its own weapons. The added maneuverability gained by eliminating a human pilot made the Lightning Bug very difficult to shoot down, able to consistently pull turns in excess of 6Gs, a feat

FIGURE 4 Two Firebees in launching position on a DC-130. These BQM-34S target drones were the precursors to the Lightning Bug, and were launched in the same manner. Department of Defense photo, in the public domain, sourced from Wikipedia.

no piloted aircraft could match.[24] Deployed in Southeast Asia, the drone was preprogrammed on the ground, most often launched in the air from under the wing of a DC-130 cargo plane. It could fly a mission with a range of 1,200 miles, and then would deploy its parachute and be recovered at sea, or snatched from the air by helicopter. It could also be launched from the ground using a booster rocket.

Lightning Bugs would take the first photos of SA-2 missile emplacements in North Vietnam, and be the first to identify MiG-21 aircraft and Russian helicopters in the country. The most successful Lightning Bug flew 68 missions without mishap or being shot down.[25] The Lightning Bug was the first drone to launch a missile, tested with both Maverick electro-optical missiles and "Stubby Hobo" glide bombs. During testing the drone's missile hit its target dead-on, guided via TV camera radio link by operators aboard airborne DC-130s and on the ground.[26] These systems were never used in combat, because the optics technology was not good enough to see camouflaged targets. A version using infrared cameras was developed, but the Vietnam War ended before it could be perfected and fielded.[27]

The Lightning Bug program would be discontinued after the end of the Vietnam War. The need for quick-response reconnaissance and electronics intelligence was reduced, and satellite reconnaissance technology was becoming reliable enough to manage strategic reconnaissance.[28] There were other drones in development programs, some of which saw covert service—such as the Sky Owl, which flew in covert US military operations in Central America in the 1980s. Some Lightning Bugs would continue to serve, flying in combat into the Gulf War, but this would be the end of major development for jet-propelled drones until contemporary times.[29]

Drones began staging a comeback in the 1980s, when low-cost models proved valuable for short-order tactical reconnaissance. The Israelis first deployed small, propeller-driven, remote-piloted vehicles carrying video cameras. During Israel's 1982 war in Lebanon, the aircraft Scout and Tadiran Mastiff were deployed at front-line locations, providing a good source of tactical information for ground forces.[30] The American military worked with Israel Aircraft Industries to develop their own version, called the RQ-2 Pioneer. The Pioneer went into service in the 1993 Gulf War, launching from warships to provide targeting information for large naval guns.[31] The AeroVironment FQM-151 Pointer, a drone small enough to be carried in a backpack and hand-launched, also saw service in that war.[32]

Countless additional drones were tested by various militaries around the world during the late 1980s and 1990s, but the drone to cement a pivotal role for unpiloted aircraft in the US military was the General Atomics Predator. First entering regular service in 1995, the Predator could fly to 25,000 feet, and stay in the air for 40 hours.[33] That ceiling was eventually increased to 45,000 feet and the remote-control link updated to satellite radio, through which it transmits video footage back to the pilot and sensor operator even as they sit at the controls halfway around the world.[34] In 2001 the Predator was outfitted with Hellfire missiles, guided from the drone to the target by laser, controlled by the sensor operator via radio link.

FIGURE 5 MQ-1 Predator. Predator is shown here on a Naval training mission in 1995, flying over the aircraft carrier USS *Carl Vinson*. Department of Defense photo by Petty Officer 3rd Class Jeffrey S. Viano, US Navy, in the public domain, sourced from the Department of Defense.

Still in service today, and joined by many other configurations and models, the bulbous nose of the Predator remains the quintessential image of the drone in the minds of the public. We have idealized the Predator as the paradigm of all drones, attributing its unique features to "the drone" in general. From the first effective gunpowder ballistics, to replaceable parts, to military aircraft, to satellites, drones are part of the evolution of a military technology lineage that created the drone as a unique, unmistakable technological weapon. Any drone narrative that we build must begin here, and looking at the drone, we can see this entire history, cast backward from its form like a shadow.

3 THE COMMERCIAL DRONE (OR, THE HOLE WHERE IT OUGHT TO BE)

Where the military drone has a specific history, the commercial drone leaves an enigmatic empty hole. The drone was invented by the military-industrial complex to be an automated aerial platform for camera equipment and other payloads. Even sold as a toy, it still fits that original mold. While there have been some interesting technological developments in drone research by nonmilitary sources, the military development legacy overwhelms nearly all civilian influence. The entirety of the drone market is oriented toward only three general uses—military, photography, and hobby—and the first category is greater than the latter two, by magnitudes. There are many speculative narratives of what a commercial drone might do in the future, but they are almost entirely removed from the facts of drone technology in the present. The commercial drone is a speculative technology that has yet to be developed, for an application that has yet to exist. And furthermore, this speculative drone is surrounded by a barrier of problems—at least eleven uniquely identifiable technological problems, stemming directly from the current state of drone technology, which must be solved if commercial drones are to succeed. For now, the commercial drone narrative is a footnote to military drones, though an important footnote we will investigate.

A brief history of multirotors

Drones available for commercial sale tend to be of quadrotor or other multirotor configuration, which are much cheaper and easier to fly than helicopters, and have slower flight and hover capabilities than fixed-wing aircraft. The quadrotor configuration is a relatively recent innovation. Working multirotor helicopters first flew back in the 1920s, but to miniaturize and stabilize the technology required technical advances only acquired recently.[1]

The multirotor is inherently less stable than a single rotor or counter-rotating, coaxial helicopter. In a quadrotor, two sets of two propellers spin in opposite directions, one set countering the rotational force of the other. By slowly accelerating or decelerating one set of rotors, the craft can yaw and roll side to side. But any sudden drop of power in a propeller can cause the craft to spin out of control. Precise control requires good electric motors, and a computer to balance the speeds in response to the motion of the aircraft. If this can be done, multirotors allow the drone to generate more lift with smaller motors and less battery power. The recent development of this automated stabilization technology is what has allowed multirotors to explode onto the scene.[2]

The Roswell Flyer was the first commercial, remote-controlled quadrotor, designed by Mike Dammars in 1991. It first sold in 1999 for $350, and was popular with hobbyists despite being made out of thin foam that didn't stand up to repeated use, leading a number of owners to engineer their own replacement airframes from carbon fiber.[3] Not unlike the first cars, early quadrotors required a tinkerer's mindset to enjoy. The DraganFly company bought Rosewell Flyer in 1999, and began selling that quadrotor under their own name along with a number of other remote-controlled hobbyist vehicles. Today they've advanced upon the design, and have a number of quadrotor models with different payload capabilities.

Universities are a powerful source of quadrotor research, especially in the field of software. Johann Borenstein began a project called HoverBot at the University of Michigan in 1992, which was a test platform for software to control a variable-pitched quadrotor for stable flight.[4] A team at Queensland University was also developing a quadrotor during the mid-1990s, as was the Experimental Rocket Propulsion Society.[5] The Mesicopter at Stanford in 1999, which developed a very small quadrotor of only two-and-a-half centimeters across, was a major advance in small propeller research. Cornell University's Laboratory for Intelligent Vehicles first made a prototype quadrotor in 2000, which was then improved upon in graduate work by Eryk Brian Nice in 2004.[6] Also in 2004, Stanford researchers built the Stanford Testbed of Autonomous Rotorcraft for Multi-Agent Control, or STARMAC, which would test and refine algorithms for flight control. MIT launched the SWARM Health Management project in 2006, which developed software for flying multiple quadrotors under the control of a single operator, and the University of Pennsylvania's General Robotics, Automation, Sensing, and Perception lab, or GRASP lab, has been flying quadrotors in tight formation around obstacles since 2010.[7] Like in the computer industry, the relationship between operating software and hardware never develops fully in-house. As yet, there is no "MS-DOS of drones" of "IBM PC standard," but without the integration of developments from numerous sources, each new multirotor project would be forced to reinvent the wheel, so to speak.

In the last few years, quadrotor sales have expanded, and there are a number of companies selling full systems ready for flight photography, aerial mapping, and hobbyist uses. There is also a growing hobbyist or DIY scene. The website DIYDrones organizes clubs and other hobbyist organizations that work on projects using open-source computer components like Arduino. That site was founded by Chris Anderson, the CEO of 3D Robotics, a company that sells drone kits, both quadrotor and fixed wing, as well as autopilot units and software for people who want to build their own autonomous vehicle. With the installation of these open-source software and components by hobbyists, nearly any vehicle can be a drone. Anderson himself has drawn parallels between his industry and the early days of hobbyist-led personal computing.[8]

Perhaps the most well-known commercial drone company today is Parrot. Parrot is a cell-phone-accessory manufacturer that produced the Parrot.AR, a $300 quadrotor that can

FIGURE 6 Parrot.AR drone. One of the most common and affordable hobbyist quadrotors available. Photo by Nicolas Halftermeyer, licensed Creative Commons, sourced from Wikipedia.

be flown using a smartphone. While originally intended to supplement an augmented reality video game on the smartphone software using overlaid graphics onto the quadrotor's onboard camera feed, the Parrot.AR has become a best-selling entry-level drone for consumers. The company recently acquired SenseFly, another drone software and hardware company, to expand their offerings in the commercial drone market. These models represent the most consumer-ready models, the point at which drones are ready to fly right out of the box.

Military-industrial companies like General Atomics, Lockheed (which purchased Ryan in 1999), and Boeing absorb the vast majority of the money being spent on drone technology. However, the US military has been trying over the years to favor smaller companies, less ensconced in the military-industrial complex, for development contracts.[9] If smaller technology companies are able to break into the business of the military-industrial complex, a unified drone industry that could cater more evenly to both civilian and military markets might develop.

The US military has stated goals of developing what they call "Future Combat Systems," which rely on cutting-edge technological improvement in six general areas: sensors, networking, robotics, armor, munitions, and hybrid power.[10] To find innovative solutions in these areas, the military might very well seek contracts with cell phone companies, software companies, or computer manufacturers—companies that could straddle the current divide between developing for military contracts and developing for civilian markets. Technology that has moved from the defense sector to the commercial sector can be more beneficial to the military, utilizing both the research and development funds of the military and the scale of commercial markets.[11] For instance, during the Gulf War, 90 percent of the GPS units used by US personnel were commercial, off-the-shelf units rather than encrypted military units.[12] GPS, a military technology, was in such high demand that the production scale of commercial industry was more important than the hardened encryption of military-grade technology. But whether or not the government allows the drone industry to mirror this pattern remains to be seen.

What are commercial drones for?

Because military drones continue to earn most of the money, most drones in development still resemble military hardware. This is where drones differ from the narratives of the automobile and the aircraft. Those technologies found commercial niches much more quickly. As of now, drone companies orient themselves into three simple categories: military use; photography use stemming directly from a military reconnaissance heritage; and hobby use, which is still fairly similar, albeit with cheaper, less advanced technology.

Military-category drones, even those available for civilian purchase, are easily identified by their expensive and powerful hardware. These drones have the ability to carry larger payloads, capture high-quality images and relay them to the operator live, and may be equipped with infrared cameras and other specialized sensors. Police forces are often the targeted consumers of these drones, or other specialized security-oriented companies. These are drones that are to be applied to a "mission" and are meant to offer strategic and tactical value—just like military aircraft.

Photography drones, while often quite high-end, differ in that they are marketed as a replacement for expensive camera aircraft to those who need high-quality imagery. The emphasis in marketing is on high-quality images and maneuverability as well as compatibility with film-grade imaging technology, rather than tactical responsiveness. These drones also are pushing into the mapping and Geographic Information Systems (GIS) market, using software to make large composite images and 3D models from collected images and GPS data. These drone models emphasize a quality of data, not a tactical superiority. And yet, their cameras make them just as capable of a reconnaissance mission as any military drone. They have not evolved significantly for us to think about them as truly unique from the military's influence, or unsuitable for that purpose.

Hobby drones fill out the roster, selling entry-level consumer systems to those who want a taste of flying a quadrotor or other small aircraft, and who might want a platform for experimenting with the technology that makes it work. Fun, durability, and adaptability are all major selling points. While this technology does not have weapons payloads and live-link satellite radios, the components are generally the same. The drone architecture is identical to a military drone, even if built from hobbyist kits.

If you ask someone in the drone industry about their potential commercial uses, you will get an entire list of possibilities. Everything from local food deliveries to lifeguarding is a potential drone task, at least in promotional media. Drones are, in the speculative narratives, everything from guard dogs, to robotic farmers, to personal companions. But it is important to recognize the difference between speculative uses for drones and actual uses for drones. Drones are a flying robotic platform—as such, there is nearly no limit of *possible* uses for them, given the advent of enabling technology. Anything we could imagine a flying robot doing is fair game for speculative narratives.

But the plausibility of aerial robots is also limited by that same technology. Quadrotors weren't quite capable of stable flight before the 1990s. The small technical advance of better electric motors and automated stabilization gave us the models we have today. Who's to say what more capable motors, better batteries, or better programming might enable in a decade? But we must be careful when dealing with plausibility. There is a high appetite in popular media for drones, analogous perhaps to Golden Age science fiction's appetite for flying cars, all-powerful electronic brains, and world-conquering robots. We must guard ourselves against vaporware—product ideas announced to stimulate commercial interest, not intended for actual production—if we want to confront the drone's limitations and see the drone narrative advance.

The drone in airspace

Cars, aircraft, and computers all took many successive modifications and breakthroughs before they could affect society on a broad scale. But there were a number of problems to be solved before this change could be considered positive. Recognizing the turbulent atmosphere that drones are entering is important—both literally and figuratively. Acceptance of drones will be contingent upon their usefulness and effectiveness, and forcing them into crowded airspace above a society where drones only cause problems will ensure a lackluster use of this technology—as was the case for civil aviation in the early twentieth century.[13]

Cars on roads did not simply act as horseless carriages, and aircraft in the skies were not cars on roads with no obstacles. Aerial robots entering the National Airspace (NAS) will not simply act as other aircraft, but will present new issues. Both the Government Accountability Office (GAO) and Congress have prepared a number of reports and hearings on the issue in recent years. The Federal Aviation Administration (FAA), the executive branch office charged with ensuring safe use of national airspace by all commercial aircraft, has limited practices for regulating safety in the case of drones. Drones have been under strict military purview and have only flown in limited-access airspace on military reservations or in foreign countries as part of military operations. And while hobbyist-style model aircraft have been permitted to fly without regulation for many years (their use described by "advisory only" FAA memo AC 91-57),[14] commercial drones are bridging the gap between model aircraft and full-sized aircraft, as well as flying in areas and under technological conditions where neither model nor piloted aircraft have previously flown.

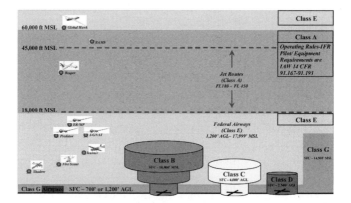

FIGURE 7 FAA airspace classification diagram. Image from Unmanned Systems Roadmap 2007–2032, produced by the Department of Defense, in the public domain.

The FAA-controlled NAS is broken down into classes. Class A is the main travel lanes for commercial jets, between 18,000 and 60,000 feet. Classes B, C, and D are the airspaces immediately surrounding different sizes of airports, dictating safe approach and departure. Class E is everything above 60,000 feet and everything below 18,000, down to roughly 700 feet above the ground (depending on the area) that is not already classed B, C, or D. Lastly, class G is everything between Class E and the ground.[15] Classes A, B, C, and D are tightly controlled by radio communications between the pilot and air-traffic controllers (ATC). Class E is less controlled, and for Class G no radio communication is required at all.

These classes are designed around what have been the common usages of the NAS. But drones change the use of this airspace. Many drones do not need airports in order to takeoff, and are capable of flying from Class G directly into Class E, and further. Some drones are easily large enough to fly into Class A, but have no pilot on board to communicate with ATC by radio.

This is only the beginning of the technological difficulties. The GAO, in a special report to Congress, identified seven major obstacles to integrating drones into the NAS.[16] They represent seven primary ways that drones differ from other aircraft technology currently in use. These seven facets represent technological holes that drone technology has yet to solve.

First, and most primary: drones do not have what is commonly referred to as "sense and avoid" capabilities, the way that pilots do. Drones are equipped with a variety of sensors, to detect all manner of things. But they do not compare to the ability of a pilot to be constantly aware of the sensory surroundings at all times while flying an aircraft. The US Army has been working on a centralized means of conducting sense-and-avoid for large numbers of drones at once using radar, but the program is still in development. A GPS-based system also seems feasible, but does not yet exist.[17]

Second are the vulnerabilities in the command-and-control system of drones. Command-and-control systems are not standardized, nor are standard fail-safes in place if the command-and-control connection is broken, in what is called a "lost-link scenario."[18] Additionally, proof-of-concept GPS-spoofing research at the University of Texas has proven that there are vulnerabilities in GPS-based guidance technology that can lead to drone hacking or other navigation failures.[19]

Third are the human factors. Flying a drone is different, and in many ways more difficult, than piloting a regular aircraft. Per a 2004 study of military data conducted by the FAA, almost 50 percent of accidents involving drones were attributed to human factors.[20] Overwhelmingly, the technology performs as it is supposed to, but challenges in human-computer interfaces led to accidents.

Fourth is simply the unreliable performance of drones. Smaller and cheaper aircraft, without the overengineering and multiplicitous safety checks of larger, human-carrying aircraft, are more susceptible to failure. What makes drones cheaper also makes them less safe.

Fifth is the lack of technical or operational standards for drones. Many smaller drones are not built by aerospace companies or designed by aerospace engineers, and they are not flown by trained pilots or serviced by trained mechanics.

Sixth is the current lack of regulations. The FAA makes it its business to ensure aircraft safety, and the safety records of the United States' NAS is testament to that. But with no current rules, all regulation for a technology very different than piloted aircraft will have to be built from scratch. Currently, the FAA is assigning Certificates of Airworthiness (COA) to drones on a case-by-case basis, but no firm process has been announced.

Seventh, the FAA is in the middle of transitioning to a new ATC system for piloted aircraft based on satellites rather than ground radar, called "NextGen." Where drones fit into NextGen is anyone's guess—perhaps this transition will solve some of the problems, but no one has described how. Congress had ordered the FAA to be ready to transition drones into the NAS by 2015, but even in that short period drone technology could change significantly.

Here we will add four additional concerns with drone technology. Not described in the GAO report, these are not technical issues with drones integrating with aircraft in the NAS, but of technical drones interacting with the public.

Eight is the issue of privacy. The FAA has refused to deal with the question of drones and privacy, deeming it outside of its jurisdiction. However, if drones are equipped with a wide range of sensors, the inevitable question is: what happens with this data once it is collected?

Nine is the issue of jobs. With all automation, there is a public fear that humans will lose their jobs as machines take over. Drone technology is often marketed as a cheaper alternative to piloted aircraft. Automation often decreases the number of humans needed for any given industry. And yet, many operators are required to keep drones in the air. The question of what such widespread aerial automation will do to the workforce is a public concern, but the answer to the question is not yet clear.

Ten is the issue of militarized technology. The drone has not significantly evolved from its military roots. Whether or not the drone is put in the air for an ostensible military purpose, it can still fulfill those same functions, and often does, even if the images it captures are meant for mapping rather than bombing, and even if the payload it drops is not explosive. What will be the short and long term effects of offering a new class of pseudo weapons in a commercial market?

And eleven is the cultural symbol of the drone. The drone has the appearance of a weapon, and it is known to be a robot. The advent of drones in the NAS means potentially thousands of weapon-looking robots confronting the public on a regular basis, even if benevolently. How will perceptual issues affect the transition, and society as a whole?

If the military narrative gives us the background on the drone's past technological development, the commercial narrative informs us of the challenges for future development. The drone's narrative extends from the past and its military roots, to the present and a host of new technological and social problems. Speculation might excite our narrative, but understanding the actual position of the drone in technological history will give us a much better footing for the next steps.

4 BLINKING LIGHTS

We tend to simplify our historical stories into straight lines, from point A to point B. The car changed society from the ground up; the Wright Brothers invented the airplane; computers give us quick access to information; robots make our lives safer, less drudge-filled, and cleaner. But these are simplifications. What we believe to be a straightforward narrative of invention is really multiple inventions that collapse into a single unit, with competing designs that coexist for a time, with the intended use of a technology supplemented by a completely different, unexpected use. History is intractably complicated. And yet we use these simplified narratives, because they are as easily deployed as a dosing rod. If you follow a dosing rod and happen to find water, then congratulations, the rod has worked. If history has a straight-line motion, and we believe we traveled that vector simply because we arrived at the end point, then the future should be no problem and we need to simply stay the course. The drone is in danger of becoming one of these simplified narratives. But while it seems that the drone will definitely do *something* significant, we haven't done enough thinking about what that something should be, and how it will happen.

Analogy is a common tool for making sense of history. Henry Ford wanted to build the "Model T of aircraft" in the Ford Tri-Motor. Apple and Atari thought they were building the Model T of personal computers in the late 1970s.[1] In 2007, Bill Gates said that the robotics industry was developing just like the early computer industry.[2] Congress today looks at the 1981 IBM PC as a standard for military open systems development.[3] The iPhone has been called Apple's Model T, the IBM of 1984 is considered to be the Apple of 2010, and Chris Anderson of 3D Robotics thinks that today's drone companies are similar to the Apple of 1977.[4] Edwin Teller, the man behind the development of the hydrogen bomb, said in 1981 that unpiloted aerial vehicles were as important as radar and computers in 1935.[5]

When we list all of these comparisons together, they appear absurd. So why do we look for analogy? Historian Michael Sean Mahoney found that computer makers and programmers compared their technology to the Model T to emphasize their goals for the technology in the world. They wanted a computer than "everyone could drive." They imagined a computer in every home, easily modifiable with standardized parts, which would revolutionize not only its own industry, but all surrounding industries with its material importance.[6] The natural comparison was to the narrative of the Model T, widely understood to be the singular symbol of the automobile's revolutionary importance. For any new technology without a proven history, it is easiest to speak in analogies and emphasize similarities between it and proven, culturally relevant technology, while minimizing their differences.

We think about history as itself a machine analog—a vast network of cogs and axles that sometimes whir smoothly, and other times grind and shear. We like to see signs that history is conforming to our expectations of it, functioning according to rules so simple they might be mechanical. In 1967, Lewis Mumford theorized that human society was itself multiple machines, these "megamachines" working as combines of associated technologies and systems to accomplish various ends.[7] Any one technology might have a disproportional effect on the larger machinery of society—what historian James Burke calls in another mechanical analogy the "trigger effect."[8] We notice sudden bursts of change: an army defeated by a stirrup or longbow, the sudden application of a well-known technology in a steamboat or a train engine, or the startling loss of life that occurs in the exploited vulnerability of disease. These highly visible technologies are like dials and indicators, and if we find they line up with our presumed historical narrative, we assume that history is unfolding "all in order." When the ENIAC computer was demoed live on CBS in 1952, blinking lights were added to the top of the machine.[9] They had no function, but the television audience needed a signal to know when the machine was "thinking." We study history like a large console, with the blinking lights of invention narratives scattered across the top—so many Model Ts, Wright Flyers, and Apple Computers. A few singular inventions serve as symbols, to verify our expectation of progress, of fruitful mechanisms through which we have designed the course of history. And it is not just cutting-edge inventions that we watch. As David Edgerton notes in his book *The Shock of the Old*, it is often an older, well-used technology that adds up to a lasting symbolic effect, whether it is corrugated iron, concrete, or the wheel, all of which transformed the twentieth century on a basic level, even though we think of these technologies as far older. What we notice in history often depends on what we are looking for, and what sort of symbol we choose, based on our present narrative.

But what we find is that the Model T, or any other blinking-light technology, is not the perfect symbol of progress we wish it to be. We deploy an image. "The Model T: an important 20th century invention." But the success of the Model T was dependent upon so many historical factors and contextual systems that to think of it as a singular device is to completely misunderstand its narrative, both on its own and as part of a larger whole.

Consider the accumulation of the following facts. The Midwest's tough roads provided for gasoline engines' success over electric and steam. Large quantities of hardwood trees in Michigan and Ohio made for a booming horse cart industry, whose workers were easily suited for adapting to automobile manufacture.[10] The large, concentrated number of nascent automobile manufacturers in Detroit and the rest of the Midwest borrowed and stole ideas from each other in a professional milieu of diffused and yet rampant technological innovation.[11] The Model T was not the first invention of Ford but only one of many designs. The car sold so widely not because it was perfect, but because Ford could actually manufacture enough of them to meet demand. The Model T could be manufactured on such a scale because with Ford's assembly line, they could make and sell a single car within the 30–90-day outsourcing billing cycle, so the parts could be made by other companies, assembled, and the car sold to the customer before Ford's own bills came due.[12] The trademark Model T was black because it was the only paint color that would dry fast enough to keep up with the assembly line process.[13] Customers could only afford the car because of the rise of consumer credit.[14] Ford could only staff its assembly lines efficiently by exploiting accessible workers in a wave of countrywide urbanization. The engineering of the assembly line was itself an invention years in the making. And the Model T might well have been the eventual undoing of the company's hegemony, because the assembly process was so overdesigned as to make the retooling of the factory for the next model, the Model A, terribly costly.

The Model T was as much an evolutionary accident as invention. Ford put off development of the next model for years, because he figured he had already invented the perfect car—so why make another? But there is no timeless invention, only contextual niches: for a period of time, all the slots lined

FIGURE 8 Ford magneto assembly line. Seen in 1913, this was the first Ford assembly line, and the first in the world, allowing the Model T to be manufactured on unprecedented scales. Photo is in the public domain, sourced from Wikipedia.

up in a row, the cylinder clicked into place, and the Model T spread across the nation in a large black wave.

If the goal is, as Michael Sean Mahoney noted, to provide a model for technology's design and use in the world, invention narratives like the Model T are only helpful by way of the most caricatured analogy. Analogy must always be detangled from how the historical narrative has been molded to the model of the blinking light—the symbolic single technology signifying invention and progress.

Invention maintains the logic of a certain historical narrative: everything is working in order, invented in its particular place and time, blinking on and off just as it was designed. But history is not designed. It is a tumultuous stream of many contradictory technologies at odds with each other, interacting with each other and with everything else, even as new designs deploy into the field.

The drone does not exist as a singular technology. Like the Model T it is a figment, a contemporary narrative borrowed from the past, by way of analogies to other misunderstood technologies. The subsystems that make the drone are a range of aeronautical, computer, and automation technologies. We give the drone a singular existence to hide its complications. We make it into something with amazing potential to hide the fact that we don't really know where it is going. We highlight its possibilities, in order to ignore all the problems we haven't yet figured out.

And yet, drones very much exist. They are the idealized symbol of technological progress *par excellence* for the twenty-first century, because like the Model T, they are an instance of a multiplicity of subsystems coming together to form an unprecedented niche. We can see that the drone has the potential to be one of these fundamental narratives when, from some future time, we look back on the present. But we cannot simply accept drones as a singular entity that will change the world in a predestined way. The Model T as America's revolutionary car, the aircraft as the realization of the dream of an airborne society, or the computer as electronic brain, the robot as godly wizardly or human hubris—these singular approaches tell only a small part of how a technological system came to be so important. Starting with the blinking light of the drone, we begin to analyze how the technologies behind it have created the circumstances to which we must respond.

5 SOFTWARE AND HARDWARE

Looking underneath the hood, we can get an idea of how the drone works now and how it might change. Each component of a technology has its own narratives. In order to better understand the drone, we have to look not only at the details of the drone as its own technological system, but at each of the technological subsystems as well. In these design specifics lie the details of why this technology is important and how we ought to use it. Amid the technological components, we also find the *ethical* component—the inimical responsibility to positively affect the use of a technology in its design.

The anatomy of the drone

Structure

The construction of the airframe is a crucial process in any aircraft, from the Wright Brothers' experiments, to the shortages of hardwood and sealing dope that dogged World War One aircraft manufacture in the United States, to the advanced composites used today. The first commercial drones, like the Draganflyer, were made of foam in order to be light enough to get off the ground. Carbon fiber or plastic is often used now, and some hobbyists are experimenting with additive manufacturing materials, in order to make rapidly prototyped drones using 3D printing. Military-grade

FIGURE 9 Tethered Aerostat Radar System (TARS). This aerostat is used by the US Customs and Border Patrol, and is equipped with radar that can see ground traffic. Photo is by the US Customs and Border Patrol, and is in the public domain.

drones are often made of Kevlar or other strong, synthetic material. The US military is also experimenting with various pressurized, structure-based (PSB) technologies. Not unlike balloons, PSBs combine other flying technologies with helium and inflated structures to keep sensor platforms in the air longer. Aerostats (balloons with long range cameras, missile/mortar detection sensors, and over-the-horizon radar) have already been widely deployed at bases in Afghanistan, and will soon be aloft over military facilities in Maryland.[1] Any new breakthroughs in materials for drone airframes could allow them to fly longer and farther, providing new shapes and profiles. Stealth materials are also relevant to drones—the military's secretive RQ-170 and RQ-180 aircraft are rumored to be made of materials that make them nearly invisible to radar.

Motors

While there are a few jet-powered drones like the Ryan Lightning Bug, the majority are powered by propellers, either gas- or electric-driven. These offer slower, more efficient flight. Perhaps the most fertile area for developments in propulsion is electric motors. New neodymium magnets and brushless motor design have revolutionized the abilities of small drones in the past two decades. Recent research also shows that alternating-current motors are beginning to have an advantage over direct-current motors, especially in very small aircraft of the hobbyist size, because their higher speed and power-to-weight ratio allow the designer to forgo the use of a gear box on the propellers, which lowers weight, vibration, and noise.[2] However, DC motors are still used widely, because they make electric systems small and inexpensive.

Batteries

The only batteries for electric drones in the 1990s were nickel–cadmium-based, because they provided enough energy release to allow a quadrotor to get off the ground. The invention of lithium-ion battery packs allowed longer flights, but these batteries would often get hot, and were known to explode. Nickel–metal hydride batteries became the best for energy density in the early 2000s, but were difficult to find in good quality at low prices. Lithium-ion batteries have since improved, and are used in many consumer drones for their ease of recharging and long life, just as in cell phones. The lithium-ion battery on the hand-launched military drone Raven, for example, will fly for 60–90 minutes on a charge. Newer lithium–sulfur dioxide batteries for that same model will allow a flight of 80–110 minutes.[3] Battery technology is perhaps most limiting for small drones, because increasing the size of the battery drastically increases the weight of the drone, requiring more thrust, and accordingly, using more power.

Battery-powered drones therefore tend to be very light, and any drone over 5 pounds will typically burn fuel, requiring liquid storage capacity. Therefore, there is a split in drone taxonomy, between small electric drones and larger fuel-burning drones. A new technological breakthrough in this area could change drone design drastically.

Propellers

Variable-pitched propellers were commonly used in aviation prior to the introduction of small drones—these allowed changes in thrust without drastic changes in engine speed. However, programming a small drone to stabilize with variable-pitch rotors requires extra weight for gearing, and sophisticated programming.[4] Newer electric motors give the ability to change speed rapidly, and so fixed-pitch propellers are now the quadrotor standard.

For very small drones, aerodynamics creates new challenges. The Stanford Mesicopter team had to start from scratch, much like the Wright Brothers, when designing propellers for their small quadrotor, only two-and-a-half centimeters long. Their fixed-pitch propellers required inventing entire new manufacturing methodology to be able to accurately shape a blade only 100 microns thin. A 2011 study by the Army Research Lab also showed that in urban areas, there are large turbulence issues for micro UAVs due to changing wind direction, more than changes in speed. Conditions like these affecting small drones are not yet understood as they are for larger aircraft. In fact, the ARL determined in the study that they did not have any equipment on hand that was sensitive enough to measure the turbulence any lower than a resolution of 10 centimeters—four times the size of the Mesicopter design. But the fact that small animals and insects can routinely navigate this sort of turbulence led the ARL to look optimistically at possibilities for future microdrones.[5]

Sensors

The information a drone can process autonomously is only as good as its sensors. These sensors can be as diverse as visible cameras, infrared cameras, laser rangefinders (LADAR), sound ranging (SONAR), GPS, accelerometers, acoustic arrays, and other positioning systems based on RFID, Bluetooth, or Wi-Fi radio signals. Each type of sensor has its strengths and limitations. GPS is very easy and fairly accurate, but can only communicate with satellites while outdoors. LADAR is very accurate indoors, but the sensors are heavy and expensive. Combining systems currently gives the best results, and enables a drone to do what is called SLAM—Simultaneous Localization and Mapping—in order to navigate with minimal help from human operators. Any improvements in sensors, even small reductions in weight and cost, would allow drones to fly much more autonomously.

Software

The information collected by a drone's sensors is only as useful as its algorithms. Automation programming is improving greatly, as universities, commercial interests, and the military all work on their own specific-use cases, developing software to suit specific types of drones in specific tasks. For all of them, automation is the key goal. The GRASP Lab at the University of Pennsylvania has made significant progress in "swarm" flying, while the military designs autopilots to fly around inclement weather, and automation to allow human operators to control multiple drones at once. At the moment, programming these acrobatics is only possible for specific drones, and software designed for swarming a particular quadrotor will not work on other models. But as the fundamental physics and techniques are improved, the possibility of cross-platform drone software is an interesting prospect.

Controllers/Interface

Despite breakthroughs in automation, drones are still very much human-controlled. And despite all the rhetoric about drones being "video game-like," flying a drone is no easy task, and each drone is different. These are real aircraft of diverse design that must rely upon real aviation principles in order to stay in the air. The military has done the most rigorous testing on controller interfaces and human workload abilities, and knows the reality of this challenge. As of 2004, almost 50 percent of military drone accidents were attributable to human factors.[6] In these cases, the aircraft performed as designed, but not as expected.[7] Improvements to controller interfaces can help reduce such failures. For example, depending on the aircraft and its control features, sometimes it is better to give the pilot an "egocentric" view, as if s/he were in the plane. Other times an "exocentric" view, as if the pilot were on the ground watching the plane, works better. Workloads for drone pilots tend to spike dramatically at particular moments—landing and takeoff in particular are much more difficult than level, steady flight. New interfaces and software that can tackle these specific pressures are not the technological breakthroughs we think about when we imagine "a robot army," but these mundane decisions about joystick placement and attitude indicators can mean the difference between a successful drone design and a dangerous crash.

Parts and wholes

Software is the part of the computer that completes defined tasks; hardware is just the physical storehouse of that programming. But, as Michael Sean Mahoney writes, "we do not interact with computers by reading programs; we interact with programs running on computers."[8] In all technology there is a complicated web of interactions between systems and subsystems. Reality is holistic—we cannot take a part out and expect things to remain the same. Our sense of the whole is changed by the contribution of the components. In any technological system, each part has its own story to tell, and we hear all the components creating their elements of the overall drone narrative, in chorus.

It was the design of Nicholaus Otto's four-stroke engine that would set the trajectory for the automobile engine, in combination with the wider availability of gasoline in the Midwestern United States and Gottlieb Daimler's engine design improvements. This component finds its obvious parallel in the propulsion unit of the drone, that has evolved from the propeller of the Radioplane to the jet of the Lightning Bug, back to propeller of the Predator, and to jet again in the Global Hawk drone, as each new application finds its best form of power. It was the Systeme Panhard that put the engine in front on the longitudinal axis. This is not unlike the shift to quadrotor design for light, cheaper drones—although all larger drones continue to be fixed-wing for stability and efficiency.

We should not forget Charles Kettering's electric starter, which made it possible for people to actually start a gasoline car without breaking their arms. This is an interface advance, which is a crucial component of drone design. From plate-glass processing, to all-steel construction, to ethyl gasoline, small technological and manufacturing innovations changed the fundamental nature of what the car *is* through history, even though the car has been running ceaselessly on roads for over 100 years. We can see similar developments in drone components through manufacturing advances, which affect propeller design, carbon fiber airframes, and lithium-ion batteries.

In inventing the airplane, it wasn't until the Wright Brothers stopped simply trying to make "a machine that would fly" and figured out some basic aeronautical math, that they could actually build an airplane. New experimental algorithms for automation and stabilization go into drones' technological mélange, today. And yet, with all this technical expertise, the Wrights' wing-warping control surface was just good enough to prove the concept. It was Glenn Curtiss and Alexander Graham Bell's invention of the aileron, an entirely new control-surface design, which would end up being the model for aircraft control surfaces through contemporary times. Multirotors depart from that tradition, using their gyroscopic forces to hover and yaw in place. But will drones go in that direction, or maintain the fixed-wing domination of aircraft? Balloons and helicopters are both minor chapters in aviation history—aerostats and multirotor designs might only be a temporary anomaly. The design that will eventually be the best fit for most drones is still being discovered.

It was military research and expensive government R&D programs that allowed aircraft engineering to advance through the twentieth century, just as it funded early computer work. Charles Babbage could have, theoretically, built a computer in the nineteenth century, had he not been stalled by engineering limitations. To what degree is the drone anchored to a particular place or time? The Lightning Bug drone successfully fired air-to-surface missiles in the 1970s, but camera technology was not good enough to make this tactically useful. But in 2001, the 30-year-old Hellfire missile took to the Predator drone as if invented for it. In the 1950s, large mainframes were still not very practical for most businesses. But as military research miniaturized electronics into transistors and integrated circuits for missile technology, computers shrunk as well, to the point where business acumen and consumer demand could take over. We see the same in drones, where miniaturization of GPS and other sensors have allowed consumers to have choices that are bringing drones closer to being a potentially viable commercial product, even if the demand does not yet exist.

The open standardization of the IBM PC allowed development on a scale that was in many ways analogous to the Model T. If not for the rush to get the IBM PC to market, it might have had a closed design. Other open protocols in computer design, like the Universal Serial Bus (USB), and many of the standards of networking technology have allowed computers to do incredible new things in concert with each other. In the push to get drones ready for use in the national airspace, it may be that open standards for sense-and-avoid and command-and-control technologies allow drone interaction in ways as unpredictable as the internet was in the early 1980s.

The Lightning Bug, the first jet-powered military reconnaissance drone, is incredibly different from modern drones. It was programmed completely in advance—and so in this sense, it was even more autonomous than the Predator drone of the 1990s. However, it could not deviate from its programmed course. Versions of the Lightning Bug were made that could be guided by television camera, by a pilot in a nearby plane operating the Bug by remote control. And Lightning Bugs were deployed in the Gulf War, some thirty years after their first development, fitted with GPS. The vast, unpredictable field of subsystem development changes the shape of a technology significantly, even as it ages. Everything from cell phone battery innovations, to 3D printing, to legislation of the national airspace, to workplace rules for welding robots could effect what drones of the near future will look like, and will be rolled into our idea of what a drone is.

Ethical components

The eventual goal for robots is to make them more autonomous. It is too difficult for a human operator to control all the aspects of servos, motors, sensors, and navigation—our ability to interface with so many subsystems is limited. To achieve precision they must be automated, so we can focus on the system as a whole. But this automation, while solving certain design problems, introduces new problems.

Automation takes away our direct control—and we don't know all the ways in which this might be a good or a bad thing, because it is still a new technology.

We want robots to be useful, efficient, easy, and like any other piece of technology, ethical. But to program an "ethical component" for a robot is no small task. Given that we have a natural ethical component to our personalities, it is tempting to leave the ethics to humans, and to focus on other components of robot design. But that doesn't mean that humans can or will always hold the ethics of robots' use in check. If drones crash due to human factors, humans might not always be the best governors for technology. As Colin Allen and Wendell Wallach said, "that human comprehension outstrips some rule-based systems is uncontroversial. That it outstrips all rule-based, algorithmic systems is less obvious to us."[9] Regardless of whether it has an ethical component to its programming or whether we leave ethics out of the design on purpose, the robot will have an ethical effect in the world. Millions have been killed in car crashes. Aircraft are used specifically to kill. Computers build hydrogen bombs and aim missiles. We know this, and we're still surprised that new technology always has ethical implications. The ethical interaction between automated systems and humans must be designed carefully and deliberately.

In a report on the development of drone interfaces, the Army Research Lab noted that technology develops in terms of "push," "pull," and "contextual" factors.[10] Push factors are driven by the technology itself—for example, developing ethyl gasoline to reduce engine knock, a problem that arose specifically in gasoline engines. Pull factors are social and cultural issues that pull a current technology into new uses. We might look at the development of the Lightning Bug, an unpiloted alternative to losing human pilots in the U-2 spy plane, as an example of a response to a pull. And contextual factors are the specifics of organizational, economic, and other systemic issues that create the terrain on which the technology exists. Technological ethics are not an activist issue, or a future issue—but the systemic terrain that exists when you develop technology in the midst of a human population. The issue is already here, and is a part of the drone, as it is in any technology.

The first makers of automobiles certainly didn't envision safety belts and traffic signals. Luckily, someone else did, but that doesn't mean those dangers weren't present from the start. It wasn't until 1966 that there was the National Traffic and Motor Vehicle Safety Act. The Federal Aviation Act wasn't passed until 1958. There are arguably few up-to-date laws about computer crime and computer-user rights on the books. And the FAA is trying to come up with drone regulations even now, as we will see in a few chapters. Whether from external regulations or from internal technological systems, engineering controls over the technology are necessary.

As different as the Lightning Bug is from the Predator, will the Predator be from future drones. We know the way that subsystems have affected the larger technological narrative in the past, and in the critical components by which drones take their current form, we can see where important innovation will likely occur. It may very well be that the invention narrative for some new, ubiquitous application of aerial robots will identify its creation not in the design of a flying machine, but in the chemical process that formulates a new type of battery, or in a program including a unique bit of code. And it may be that whatever determines what drones are eventually "for" remains to be discovered in the unexpected advances or detriments contributed by one of these subsystems.

6 THE NON-DRONE

What is it about an aerial robot that earns such distinct attention? If the drone narrative is simply a composite of its component technologies, what is it that makes it unique, and worthy of the name "drone"? Why is an aerial robot called a drone, but a digital camera or self-driving car is not? When we talk about the intended uses for these non-drone technologies we find they often play similar roles as drones; but when not aboard an aerial robotics platform, they aren't included in the narrative of the drone.

By looking at these non-drone technologies, we can see the edges of a definitional narrative. The drone is something specific, and not all technology qualifies. There is a symbolic weight to the definition of the drone. The drone means more, and that is why it has become so important to our contemporary society.

Surveillance

If we look at what are commonly called drones, there is one feature we see in almost every situation—the presence of a camera. Humans are a visually oriented species. When we create a flying robot, one of the first things we want to do is put a camera on it. This allows us to use our sense of sight to help control the craft, and to use the information from the camera for tactical purposes. Along with the other sensor technology that makes drones possible, microelectronics have allowed digital cameras to become smaller and lighter, to the point that putting one on a small quadrotor is now trivial. But it wasn't always this way. The first spy satellite to carry an electro-optical imaging system was the KENNAN KH-11, launched by the US National Reconnaissance Office (NRO) in 1976. Previously, spy satellites were disposable, using giant film cartridges that were ejected out of the spacecraft to parachute down to earth, to be snatched out of the air by a plane. This orbiting digital camera sensor, although used in conjunction with a powerful telescope, had a resolution of only 800 pixels by 800 pixels, or 0.64 megapixels.[1] Today, it is common for smartphones to have cameras with over 8 megapixels. Drones have very similar, if not identical equipment.

Digital closed-circuit television cameras (CCTV) are now ubiquitous, benefiting from cheap camera sensors as well. CCTV is found on ATMs, storefronts, traffic signs, and vehicles. Automated License Plate Recognition Systems (ALPR) are a more sophisticated application—a series of infrared cameras mounted on a car or stationary structure, ALPR can scan and record over 1,800 separate plates per minute, and then check them against a database.[2] Facial recognition technology is also improving, which uses

FIGURE 10 MiniHawk 2i Automatic License Plate Recognition System. Almost so small as to be unnoticeable, this camera system photographs license plates and instantly compares them against a police database. Photo is in the public domain, sourced from Wikipedia.

algorithms to detect identifying characteristics of people's faces, and look them up instantly in a similar database.

Military spy satellites also pioneered electronics intelligence (ELINT) in addition to digital photography, by scooping up ambient radio and radar waves. This technology is found on drones, but also on stationary platforms, such as a device called Stingray, which sends out a signal similar to a cell-phone tower. Nearby cell phones are fooled into connecting to it as if it were a tower, and then the Stingray can eavesdrop on the device and track its location.[3] Similar devices can do the same thing for Wi-Fi, Bluetooth, RFID and other data transmission technologies, tracking mobile devices by their unique identifiers, and often locating the devices to within mere feet.

Any of these surveillance technologies can be loaded onto a drone as easily as they can a car or a rooftop, let alone a piloted aircraft. However, we tend to think of a drone as having surveillance capabilities unique among other platforms. In congressional testimony regarding the use of drones in the United States, privacy is brought up as an issue time and again.[4] California passed legislation about the use of data collected by drones in early 2014, and many other states are considering similar laws.[5] And yet there is no similar legislation in the United States about Stingrays, ALPRs, CCTV, or other similar technologies. Somehow, the invasion of privacy by drones is considered more worthy of regulation, though the technology is very similar.

Algorithms

Without algorithms telling it how to stay in the air, a drone would be much more difficult to control. These automated programs do everything from balancing the lift and torque from rotor blades, to following preprogrammed waypoints, to running the radios that allow the drone to be in communication with its operator. From the very first gyroscopically balanced aerial torpedoes, feedback controls have been employed so that humans could step back from the basic task of keeping the robot in the air, and concentrate on other things.

But algorithms are doing more than that simply flying the vehicle. We are automating all facets of our society, from web searches to traffic light signaling to medical implants. Cars that can warn drivers of hazards are already on the market, and cars that help steer are in development. Google's famous self-driving cars have driven half a million miles without an accident, whereas the average human has an accident about every quarter million.[6] The largest passenger jets are so automated that one might consider the pilot to be the redundant safety system for the computer, rather than the other way around. The more automation, the more "human factors" accidents are reduced, whether on the internet, on the road, or in the sky.

But we don't think of a Boeing 787 as a drone, and airlines would balk at the idea of selling this idea to their customers. There is something about the aerial robot that is more independent, more invasive, more "drone-like" than any of its other automated cousins in the air, on the ground, or on our networks.

Weapons

Perhaps it is the military legacy of drones that keeps them distinct in our minds from other automated technologies.

Remote weapons, whether an arrow or a ballistic missile, always have carried a certain stigma of cowardice in the military narrative of heroism and warrior culture. That is, of course, until they are proven to win a battle, victory being the only lasting glory in violence. Drones are no more remote than the missiles and aircraft from which they were designed. The Hellfire missile used most commonly on armed drones today was originally fielded in 1982, designed to take out Soviet tanks from piloted helicopters. Even some of the most exotic automated weapons on drones were originally designed for conventional aircraft. Take the BLU-108 for example, in production since 1992, and used in the Iraq War. This anti-armor submunition is dropped in a single, glide bomb unit. A number of smaller cartridges drop out of the glide bomb, each deploying a separate parachute to drift toward the column of armor below. At about 100 feet, each cartridge fires a horizontal rocket, starting the cartridge spinning rapidly. Four discs, or "skeet," are then released from the spinning cartridge and thrown out parallel to the ground like a discus; in each skeet is an infrared camera that can detect a vehicle below. Once the camera senses that that a wobbly flying disc is pointed at a vehicle, it fires itself down toward the ground with an explosive charge, burying the explosively formed penetrator into the vehicle. From one glide bomb, an entire column can be decimated in minutes. The BLU-108 has been used to arm RQ-5 Hunter drones, but also B-52s and F-15s, planes flown for more than thirty years.[7]

FIGURE 11 F-16C launching AGM-154 Joint Standoff Weapon. The AGM-154 is one of several delivery methods developed for the BLU-108. This guided glide bomb is dropped by piloted aircraft, and can glide as many as 130 kilometers to its target. Photo is by Michael Ammons of the US Air Force, and is in the public domain, sourced from Wikipedia.

There is something uncanny to the human mind about this level of automation in war. And yet it is the drone that has become synonymous with military automation, rather than cruise missiles and smart bombs. It might not be the automation of targeting, weapons delivery, or navigation that really makes us think "drone." Perhaps it is more about the idea that choosing whether or not to fire is a decision that could be automated. Currently, the decision to fire is not automated in military drones, and the military has specifically said that it will not automate this decision. And yet, this has not allayed the public's uncanny feelings about drones.

Nearly every other aspect of the drone has been automated, in at least some cases. But the decision of whether or not to fire is very low workload compared to tasks like takeoff and landing. Nothing is out of the question for automation, and the question of automating the decision to fire could indeed crop up in the future. But would this substantially change the effect of the drone? Is it different than the detonation of a land mine or a BLU-108?

Robots

One of the easiest ways of defining drones is as *aerial robots*. There are many robots on the ground using similar technology, but we are not as quick to think of them as drones, specifically. Ground robots include self-driving cars, the industrial robots descending from Unimate, medical robots in hospitals and in service care, and military ground robots. iRobot, maker of the popular Roomba automated vacuum system, also makes the PackBot, one of the first widely deployed military robots. Light enough to be carried by a single soldier and controlled with a handset developed directly from game system controllers, the PackBot is used for reconnaissance and bomb disposal, currently in service in Afghanistan and Iraq. Meanwhile, the Roomba is the most popular service robot in the world, comprising half of their total population.[8]

FIGURE 12 Navy personnel and PackBot. This sailor is an explosive ordinance disposal technician, posing here with his PackBot. Photo is produced by the US Navy, and is in the public domain, sourced from Wikipedia.

And the cutting-edge iRobot ATRV-2 can be equipped with more simultaneous reconnaissance sensors than almost any other robot system, including: "visible camera, IR camera, laser rangefinder (LADAR), weather sensor, stereo camera pair, sound navigation and ranging (SONAR), GPS, a digital compass, and an acoustic array."[9] And yet, we tend not to refer to any of these robots as drones.

With such similiar technology features on these robots and drones, many of the same ethical questions apply. They can be just as easily armed, and carry the same surveillance packages. The question of automation for robots and drones is identical, in the minds of most ethicists, engineers, and operators. In one fundamental research paper, four levels of automation are identified: "1) information acquisition; 2) information analysis; 3) decision and action selection; and 4) action implementation."[10] Whether the robot is flying or driving, firing missiles or doing surgery, sensing with SONAR or with LADAR, the questions are the same—which tasks should be automated, and which should not? When should unpiloted systems be used, and when should they not?

And yet, drones do differ from the rest of these robots in our apprehension of them. In a flying robot, there is something removed, something remote. SWORDS—tracked military robots fitted with cameras, machine guns, and grenade launchers—have been deployed by the US military in combat, but they aren't very useful. They are jokingly referred to by US troops in East/Central Asia as "Taliban Resupply

Vehicles," because enemy fighters will sneak up on them, simply tip them over, and take the weapons.[11] This dumb, automated machine does not exhibit drone-like behavior. We think of drones moving in ways that humans cannot. Consider a missile that flies with acceleration no human could survive. Think of a surveillance drone that remains on station for forty hours at a time, or a tiny quadrotor that flies through an open window as easily as we walk down a sidewalk. There is something about flying drones that benefits from removing the human from the cockpit. These are aircraft without cockpits—not aircraft with an empty pilot seat, but aircraft that function better without pilots.

The name "drone" comes from a legacy of targeting drones, nonhuman things that could be swatted out of the sky for target practice. But when the Lightning Bug drone was developed as a reconnaissance craft, it kicked off the process of engineering vehicles to fully exploit the capabilities of automated technology. This is not simply about saving humans from the "Three D's." This is about saving the technology from dealing with *us*. Before long, the Lightning Bugs could pull more Gs than a human pilot could, and were routinely outmaneuvering the human pilots for whom they were supposed to be cannon fodder.[12]

The drone specifically refers to aerial robots for a reason—it is operating in a space that humans were not born to exist in. We may trespass in the sky by strapping ourselves into aircraft, but we are always visitors. Drones, and the automation technology they contain, operate in ways that humans never could. They are not taking our jobs so much as they are beginning to perform jobs that we never could. Automation technology will affect our society in a myriad of ways unrelated to flying robots, just as computers, aircraft, and cars all have their compound effects. There will be the essence of a drone in every traffic light, every trash can, every household appliance, and even within our own bodies, as small sensors networked to information-processing algorithms begin to process the data of our world in ways that we could never have done or imagined. But the drone narrative will be perpetually linked to the flying robot. The drone was the first robot that obviously surpassed us. Not a heavy industrial machine, or a top-heavy, trundling thing; rather, the drone buzzing over our head, within someone's control, but just out of our reach.

7 WHAT THE DRONE IS FOR

Our simplified narrative of the drone is becoming more complicated. We understand where the drone came from, what it is and isn't, and why it is unique. Now we can begin to make a list of things that the drone could be *for*—intentionally, unintentionally, and accidentally. Various speculative narratives pick up specific potentials. In our narrative of the drone, we want as many potential endings as possible, properly weighted according to their plausibility. What separates these speculative narratives from vaporware is that they are not just the future we want, but a spectrum of futures we might actually get. Just as the only way to understand the past is to look into specific details, the only way to imagine the future is by investigating specific, unexpected possible outcomes.

Intended functions

Every technological object is designed with intended functions. These are the device's purposes, what its uses are assumed to be. Of course, objects are often used for completely different purposes than they were designed for, and they do things that no one intends at all. Cars are meant to be used as transportation. But sometimes people live in them. And sometimes they crash, despite the efforts of the designer and the user to avoid this outcome entirely.

Drones, as we have seen, were originally developed with solely military functions in mind. They were used to train military pilots, to conduct reconnaissance for military operations, and eventually to deliver weapons to military targets. Given that their designers had these tasks in mind, these are the functions at which drones excel. If drones could not be effectively developed for these tasks, projects would have been canceled and drones would not have been used. Drone programs are still canceled all the time. The embattled Global Hawk program, high-altitude descendant of the original Ryan Lightning Bug drone, has faced many challenges about whether its effectiveness justifies its cost.[1]

Therefore it is no surprise that when it comes to the question "what is it for?" commercial drones largely answer in a similar manner to their military progenitors. They conduct reconnaissance and surveillance, they excel at tactical missions (but without the ordnance) and data collection, or are hobbyist drones, which we might generously call "experimental test" aircraft. Like the commercial aircraft industry, the commercial drone industry aligns itself to the source of development dollars. Without a large customer base for consumer use, the primary customer for drones of all shapes and sizes continues to be the military. Furthermore, as police forces become more militarized, adopting other armored vehicles and weaponry normally reserved for the armed forces, having a few less-lethal drones in their arsenal is not out of the question, and drone companies are certainly conscious of this.

There are signs of evolution, as commercial drones shift to adapt to the perceived intentions of customers in the market—for example, photography drones capable of camera upgrades for cinematic equipment, marketed to filmmakers as another technologically advanced piece of movie gear. This is a fairly robust and feasible purpose that has led design in a new direction. Other drones are developing tie-ins and interfaces for smartphones, taking the high-priced-gadget route to early adopters as their potential market. Even as they are true to their roots of automated, aerial camera platforms, these are perhaps the most divergent drones yet from military designs, and also most likely to find success, given the feasibility of their designed purposes and the existence of a market prepared to buy.

Potential functions

Other potentially viable commercial functions are in development, though none have proven themselves in the same way that military functions have. There is the repeating narrative of the delivery drone, bringing anything from food to mail to one's location, aiming at usurping the delivery van's century-long role in society. Very few drones have enough cargo capacity, and the airspace is too difficult to navigate with current SLAM capabilities to make this a realistic outcome. However, a brewery made headlines recently when its prototype drone delivered a small case of beer to ice fishermen on a frozen lake.[2] This attracted the legal attention of the FAA, which had not provided them with a COA for their drone—one might conclude that the FAA was attracted by the fact that this is actually a possible scheme and not purely speculative. A six-pack of beer is about the right weight for a multirotor drone, and a frozen lake is a relatively easy area to navigate, without buildings, trees, or power lines as obstacles. Still, without the safety systems used by commercial aircraft, any drone could potentially become a hazard in the airspace.

Another speculative narrative uses drones as antennas, either in a wide array or for single-repeater usage, such as to broadcast Wi-Fi signals.[3] The software research to enable this kind of use is certainly underway, and seems plausible. However, the economics of keeping drones constantly in the air to serve as antennas, rather than just erecting a tower, seems uncertain. Certainly, the military uses station-keeping drones for ELINT and other electronic coordination activities, but their budget has more capacity for such expensive operations. And even the military has begun using tethered aerostat balloons rather than drones for this kind of constant relaying and surveillance, because the physics of keeping a balloon in the air for a longer period of time are less resource-intensive than a heavier-than-air craft.

Most other speculative uses are adaptations of what drones can already do—navigating automatically and collecting images. A drone might fly ahead of you while you drive, warning you of upcoming traffic conditions. A drone might follow you, filming the motions of you and your friends and family, like a self-operating vacation camcorder. A drone might lead you to safety, on a tour, to a home for sale, or to a nearby store, all depending on where you want to go and who might want you to go there. A drone could take pictures and survey the land for any purpose in which visible imagery might be useful—farming, forestry, real estate, geographic survey, security, and so on. When it comes to aerial robotics, a camera has proven to be one of the easiest cargoes to take aloft, and so wherever drones go, imagining them carrying cameras is completely within the range of possibility. Conceiving the idea of a drone doing anything that we might do on the ground while hovering in the air is not difficult. But programming it, given the current technology, is not nearly as simple.

Unintended functions

Drones, like any technology, have unintended functions. Safety problems are unintended functions. Drones fly through the air, are capable of high speeds, and accidents do happen.

Some drones are very light; others are not. But gravity affects all objects the same, and falling from a few hundred feet, there aren't many models that wouldn't be capable of doing damage to people or property. With some rough calculations, we can determine that a 5-ounce baseball dropped from a height of 100 feet will reach terminal velocity, or roughly 74 miles per hour. This is equivalent to the speed of many major league baseball pitches, which assuredly no one would volunteer to receive in the head. Most small drones are heavier than that, and would do a good amount of damage from a reasonable height.

Safety is the primary concern of the FAA, and it is of little doubt that the FAA has been so slow in drafting rules for drone use because of the complexity of the task. There are too many unanswered questions of how safety concerns will be mitigated. It is only because of the great care taken in regulating piloted aircraft that we don't have vehicles plunging out of the sky at all times.

Security is also an issue. Much of the congressional testimony about drones entering the NAS have revolved around potential security concerns, and the lack of means for preventing these potentialities. The United States has a fascination with fantasizing potential terrorist attack schemes—ever since the 2001 terrorist attacks the media is full of stories of hypothetical attack vectors, whether it is hallucinogenic drugs in the water supply, or cargo containers full of terrorists being shipped around the country under the noses of the authorities. Very few of these security concerns ever end up threatening anyone's life, though the media culture tends not to reflect upon that statistical fact.

Occasionally, security forces themselves play into this speculation. In 2011, a Massachusetts man named Rezwan Ferdaus was arrested by the FBI and accused of plotting to fly a remotely controlled aircraft loaded with explosives at a number of targets in Washington DC.[4] The FBI suggested this plot to him through covert informants, and provided him with a model airplane (loaded with dummy explosives), then arrested him before he could do anything with it. But still, the notion that such a scheme might be plausible stuck. With drones in the sky, the fear that one of them might be carrying a bomb will surely follow, whether such an event ever occurs.

The security of the systems ensuring the safety of drone flight is a more serious concern. In 2012, Todd Humphreys, a researcher at the University of Texas, succeeded in showing how software could be used to alter the GPS signal used as a guidance reference by a drone helicopter.[5] This "GPS spoofing" was possible because civilian drones, unlike military drones, use an unencrypted GPS signal that is easy to detect and mimic. This vulnerability affects not only drones but also any off-the-shelf GPS system guiding cars, ships, or commercial aircraft. Other safety systems for drones, such as a centralized sense-and-avoid system, might also be vulnerable to any number of potential attacks and hacks, and the integrity of such systems can't be known until they are developed and released.

Last but not least, privacy concerns are an unintended consequence of drones. The ability to fly cameras through the air collecting visible light information, as well as any number of other types of information depending on the drone's sensors, means that a proliferation of this sort of data, containing potentially private information, is very likely with drones. Legally, the United States has very lax laws about what sorts of data may be recorded in public areas compared to Europe, where the legal protection of privacy is more strongly enforced. However, even the legality of a drone's data collection cannot guarantee that this aspect of drones will always function as designed. Networked data systems from ATMs to email are compromised all the time, delivering information whether it is legal or not. When that data is digitized, what is legal and illegal is often beside the point. Any system that collects data could potentially do things with the data in ways other than it was designed for, and as one more networked device, drones certainly fall into this category. The question becomes not so much about what is legal and illegal as what we consent to, and what our technology is capable of doing if our consent is ignored.

As users of drones, and as those whom drones will potentially be used on, we are forced to consider all of these potentialities, whether they are intended, possible, or unintended. The various technological subsystems that we identify as "a drone"—whether the sensors, the navigation system, the payload, or the drone's operator—have the potential to act upon us and around us in all of these ways. A drone without its propellers, camera, and GPS would not get very far, and so we would consider that to be just a collection of parts. But given its wings, eyes, and sense of direction, suddenly we might find ourselves persecuted by this object. These otherwise inert technologies, assembled together, can take a more malignant form.

The drone is a point of collision in our negotiations between our selves and our technological systems. It is the junction between the designers of drone systems and those who will have to deal with the consequences of those systems. Whether technology contributes to progress or not, we end up in a position of intersection with those systems, at which point we are forced to respond.

8 THE DRONE IN DISCOURSE

With all of the drone's speculative narratives, it's no wonder that there are many expressed opinions about the present and future of drones. We hear various disjointed aspects of the drone narrative constantly: in the news media, in congressional testimony, in books, in sales pitches, in protests, and in art galleries. The debate has little in the way of common ground, being fractured into so many opinions. We'll summarize a number of those positions, to contextualize them into our growing narrative.

The military and the government

The military is invested in drones for a simple reason: they work. And they have defended their use of drones on this basis, using the constant presence of threats to national security as the brunt of their argument. But by and large, the military does not engage in discussion of the ethics of drones, as much as they refuse to discuss the ethics of war in general, outside of their legal justifications in certain scenarios.

As aerial platforms, drones provide a cheap and relatively safe platform for reconnaissance, surveillance, and weapons delivery. Given the military's positive experience with drones thus far, they are looking to further develop and improve their results. They are developing systems useful in contested airspace, and improving automation, given that serious gains could be made in decreasing workload for the operators and improving safety records. With improved automation, ground robots might prove as useful as those in the air.

Given the aircraft's success in military missions, other agencies of government are looking to adapt them to domestic tasks. Predator drones are already being used domestically by the Coast Guard for military missions, and they are being adapted to a more policing-style mission by the Border Patrol and FBI. NASA and NOAA also employ them for research. These agencies all support drone use, but operate independent of FAA authority, or use their drones through COA permits not available to the public.

The FAA

The FAA has purview over the safety of the national airspace, and has kept its interest in and statements on drones strictly

FIGURE 13 Ikhana MQ-9. NASA purchased an MQ-9, known as the Reaper in its military variant but named Ikhana in this case, used in the Suborbital Science Program. Photo is produced by NASA, and is in the public domain, sourced from Wikipedia.

within those bounds, refusing to speculate about policy or other ethical or societal implications. Congress has had to force their hand in drone regulation, setting deadlines in the 2012 FAA Modernization and Reform Act, dictating that regulation must be in place by December 2015. Meanwhile, the independent Government Accountability Office (GAO) has filed several reports to Congress on the limited progress made. Only recently the FAA has satisfied a number of the deadlines set for it regarding drones, albeit a little late. They do provide COAs as stipulated (342 were granted to 106 different federal, state, and local agencies in the first half of 2012[1]), and recently announced the formation of six test ranges in order to work on integrating drones into the NAS.

Notably, the FAA has specifically said that they are not interested in creating rules or guidelines on privacy issues with drones.[2] As they view themselves to be concerned with safety, they have passed on the opportunity to work in this area of concern, and it remains to be seen which agency will take the lead on drone-related privacy issues.

They are, however, willing to fine individuals who attempt to fly drones without a permit. A recent $10,000 fine for flying a drone without COA was rejected on appeal to the National Transportation Safety Board. While COAs exist to allow drones, there are rules against flying drones without them. The FAA is in the process of counterappealing.[3]

Lobbyists

There is a primary trade association group for the drone industry, called the Association for Unmanned Vehicle Systems International, or AUVSI. They hold one of the biggest drone trade shows every year, and their president has been called before Congress several times to speak on the issue of drones. Their position is very consistent—they believe that drones present a large opportunity both economically and technologically, and therefore should be allowed into the NAS as soon as is feasible. As might be expected, they support a largely hands-off view of drones in the NAS, promoting the idea that manufacturers and operators themselves will take the responsibility for safety and privacy issues. They have developed their own Code of Conduct which, while stating the group's membership's commitment to protecting privacy and safety, is strictly voluntary, and does not list anything specific in terms of actions to be taken or avoided.

Businesses

Businesses echo the commercial promise of drones that AUVSI voices, but tend to stay out of legislative and regulatory matters. They are primarily interested in selling their particular products, whether they are military drones, commercial photography drones, or hobbyist models.

An interesting voice from businesses is that of proposing speculative uses for drones, whether or not these uses are realistic. By generating publicity, they can both sell their own products and services, and generate wider media interest in drones, even if the speculative concept turns out to be no more than vaporware. Take the recent hype surrounding

Amazon's "delivery drones," that would purportedly deliver packages of less than 5 pounds. This is only the most publicized concept shopped to the media of late—other concepts offered the delivery of books, or food. None of these business plans are feasible given the current state of drone technology, but as free advertising these speculative drones soar high. Another egregious example is the Silicon Valley start-up Matternet, which claims to be developing drones for "humanitarian purposes." While any reasonable person could probably theorize at least half a dozen potential "humanitarian uses" for drones, Matternet has little to show in the way of actual concepts, outside of a few test flights in 2012, a handful of drawings of drones marked with the sign

FIGURE 14 Matternet drone. The rendered mockup of the as-yet-undeveloped drone shows it flying over the wretched huts of—somewhere. Photo reproduced courtesy of Matternet.

of the Red Cross flying over dilapidated huts, and a couple of TED Talks.

News media

The news media loves drones, and reports on them widely, whether on actual events or speculative press releases. As might be expected, the news has a penchant for inflating the drama of any particular drone episode. Security vulnerabilities are a favorite in the news—any small vulnerability discovered by researchers is typically reported as affecting all drones. For example, a simple MAC address spoof on the unencrypted control interface of a Parrot.AR quadrotor was headlined as "zombie drones" run amok.[4] Todd Humphreys's research into GPS spoofing at the University of Texas was portrayed as "hacking a government drone," even though the only relationship between the proof-of-concept hack and the military was that the military provided a portion of the funding for the research.[5] The media also loves controversy—any time the FAA issues a cease-and-desist letter to a drone operator, the story is widely written up.

On the other hand, the news media has done significant work in investigating and publicizing covert military drone strikes. Without the work of groups like the Bureau of Investigative Journalism, much of the truth about the number and location of CIA targeted killings would never be known by the public.

Activists

As there are drone proponents, there are certainly also drone detractors. The group Code Pink and activist Medea Benjamin have taken the forefront in protesting drone use in the United States, showing up outside of drone trade shows to voice their opinions to industry leaders, as well as confronting elected officials. In her book, *Drone Warfare*, Benjamin outlines the full case for why military drones ought to be protested: they are expensive, they crash, they can go out of control without human pilots, they can be hacked, they miss their targets and kill civilians, they hit the wrong targets and kill civilians, they cause bad intelligence, and they have been involved in "friendly fire" incidents.[6] She enumerates the legal arguments against military drones from a number of perspectives, and furthermore decides that they are, at root, immoral and unethical means for conducting a war, due to all of these reasons.

Benjamin's arguments are not substantially different than the arguments of any anti-war protester. The military-industrial complex, supported by the broad funding of the US government, has been developing new technologies to further their military goals for many years. Ever since the Springfield and Harpers Ferry armories and the establishment of the American System of Manufacturing, military dollars have led technology industries in a war-like direction. Despite the civilian uses that might be spun out of this technology, military technology exists and is funded for one purpose, and one purpose above all. Drones are not unique from other military technology—there is no fault with drones that cannot be found with other weapons systems. However, what is interesting is the way that drones captivate the public. Drones shine a spotlight on issues of covert US military action. Drones provide a reason to ask age-old questions about technological and warfare ethics again, and to demand that public officials answer.

There is also domestic activism on the privacy front. Groups like the American Civil Liberties Union (ACLU), the Electronic Frontier Foundation (EFF), and the Electronic Privacy Information Center (EPIC) have all been involved in asking tough privacy questions about the domestic use of drones. EPIC and other organizations have petitioned the FAA to regulate drone privacy issues, and are also focused at the state and local level with the goals of limiting the ability of law enforcement to use drones for evidence collection, prohibition of general public surveillance, and limitations on the retention of data collected from drones, both commercial and governmental.[7]

Artists

Artists and writers of fiction have been making significant efforts in drawing public attention to drones and changing the conversation with their work. We'll be delving deeper into these works in the next chapter, but to briefly make the point: in addition to simply drawing attention to the debate around drones, creative artists and writers have served to make factual information about drones available for those who otherwise might not have discovered it in the news media. Also, artists are free to engage in speculation about drones without needing to support a particular business model, as commercial interests do. Artists therefore often bring a much more pessimistic, dystopian character to the discourse of drones, and therefore are a strong source of criticism.

The public

Outside of these parties, it is difficult to get a sense of what the general public thinks of drones. A 2013 Gallup survey found that 65 percent of Americans supported drone strikes on suspected terrorists abroad. 41 percent supported strikes against US citizens living abroad suspected of terrorism, 25 percent supported strikes inside the United States against terrorism suspects, and 13 percent supported strikes against US citizens suspected of terrorism inside the United States.[8] Overall, these results suggest a not-in-my-neighborhood, not-someone-like-me acceptance of military drone strikes.

In an AP-NCC poll, 44 percent of people supported the police using drones, while 36 percent were opposed. In the same poll, 35 percent said they would be concerned for their privacy if police used drones, while 36 percent said they were not concerned.[9] As the public begins to interact with drones "in the wild," we will no doubt see new types of interactions that are more enlightening of general opinion and with greater influence to the overall discourse than simple telephone surveys.

With all of these voices, we are left with a verbal sketch of a drone that is asymmetric, contradictory, and uncertain. The main problem is that these voices are talking to themselves, and not talking to each other. Anti-war activists go unheard by the military-industrial complex, government regulators cannot speak in the language of speculative commercial or artistic possibilities for the future, and the military would probably prefer to never speak to the public if it had its way. The solution is not to seek common ground, because between some of these voices there is no compromise, nor should there be. However, we should keep the drone narrative itself in common. Attempting to square any particular interested parties' ideas into a single concept is futile, but together they make up the many different ways that people are currently approaching the drone narrative. Just as we cannot treat the drone technology itself as a singular and unique system, we cannot treat any particular idea of drones as singular.

The reality of the drone is that it is quickly becoming a social narrative, and that the social conflict will be reflected in how the technology is used and conceptualized. Any objective determination of future intentions for the drone will always be channeled through this social discourse, and so it must be factored into our drone narrative.

9 DRONE FICTION

Given our emphasis on a fact-based drone narrative, it may seem odd to look at fiction. In drone fiction and art we find a social, expressive narrative of the drone. Speculative narratives of the future are one means of expressing what we think the drone will be, given our current understanding. Outside of the realm of fact lies a more personal, psychological narrative.

Fiction is a means for working out our culturally invested psychological constructions for any number of topics. Whether we are talking about novels, popular music, or cinema, the dreams and ideas of society are played out across these narratives. W. G. Sebald, in his book *On the Natural History of Destruction*, traces the way that German authors in the post–World War Two era failed to discuss the destruction wrought upon their country in their fiction. He links this to a refusal to deal with the psychological consequences of real events. But it was not just a denial, according to Sebald. They were unable to describe what they had seen, even in fictional terms, because they were focused on the task of self-definition after the terror of Nazism and the crushing blow of their country's defeat. In fixating on what came after the war, without taking up the actual damaging material of the war, the process of healing could only be half-complete. Given how complicated and contradictory the discourse on drones is, we could certainly use fiction to work out the contradictions, even if only for the brief span of a book, a song, or a film. But not wholly unlike Sebald's post-war Germany, society in the contemporary United States avoids the drone in fiction.

w/a/k *analogy*

There is science fiction, often called speculative fiction, that attempts to dream up worlds in the future, whether they are supposed to be possible, allegorical, or simply fantasy. There are drones in speculative fiction. Robots and other human-created automatons have been important features of the genre since the word was invented in 1921 by *R.U.R.*, a play about robots taking over the world and destroying humanity. But speculative fiction occurs not entirely in our world—rather, in a world that is different. It is a future or an alternate past, a world like ours but different in a few key ways. The robots of *R.U.R.* are not really machines. They are part of an allegory about the peasant class—the peasants being the source of the Czech word "robota"—more than any machine. Rather than write about class issues in the present, it is easier to deal with them in a speculative allegory, separate from our reality.

It is easier to think about robots in an allegorical, abstract-futurist reality than to deal with realistic robots in fiction. Robots are simply an existential philosophy puzzle in Isaac Asimov's Three Laws of Robotics, rather than an actual ethical question posed to designers and consumers.

FIGURE 15 1939 *R.U.R.* WPA poster. This poster was designed by the Works Progress Administration for a production of *R.U.R.* This image was produced by the Federal Government, and is in the public domain, sourced from Wikipedia.

Unimate, the industry robot system, first started taking on jobs of autoworkers in 1971, but how often do we see that story in cinema? Aerial robots kill people today, and yet it is more entertaining and psychologically easy to watch Arnold Schwarzenegger or Tom Cruise fight robots in an unfamiliar future.

Stories of automata and animate objects date back to times of the Ancient Greeks, but they were always the creations of great or wise men. The stories told of secret and powerful knowledge akin to magic bound into objects. They often coincided with the skill of flight, or of making animate insects or animals, in these wise men's abilities. As Leonardo da Vinci wrote, "A bird is an instrument working in accordance with mathematical law, which instrument it is within man's capacity to reproduce with all its movements," and this seems to be the spirit with which robots were envisioned.[1]

Around the eighteenth and nineteenth centuries, as the industrial revolution got underway, these magical objects became much more machine-like, with the power to kill and wound in gruesome ways being their primary trait, rather than accomplishing their creators' whims. The monster of Mary Shelley's *Frankenstein* and the machines of Samuel Butler's *Erewhon* made humans suffer their own technological hubris, just as in Čapek's play. This reoccurring theme in human literature is interesting in its own right, but as robots proliferate in society, we look for something more from our fiction.

The drone is beginning to build a different speculative literary heritage than its robot progenitors. While the robot is the product of knowledge, either reckless or astute, the drone is more a characterization of mystery and the unknown. The drone is deeply serious, bringing with it the politics of death. It is also cryptic, a bit beyond our understanding, within our world but outside of our vision. It is something built by humans, but humans we don't know. It is controlled by those we cannot see who hide behind officialdom and secrecy.

There is not much drone fiction currently, but perhaps it is not strange that much of what there is can be found online. There, the ease of experimentation means that new fiction can be produced, shared quickly, and find a receptive audience, as any other cutting-edge technology can.

Teju Cole's *Seven Short Stories about Drones* was originally serialized on the author's Twitter account. Each story is a brief line, pulled from a recognizable novel, rewritten to include mention of drones or military drone strikes. His lines—like some of the most memorable in literature such as the opening lines to *Moby-Dick*, *Mrs. Dalloway*, and *The Stranger*—pull the reader out of social media stupor to think critically about drone strikes, with the suddenness of an actual missile falling from the sky. The lines also turn back on the history of literature, to ask us about novels from another time and place: a novel of revenge, of a suicide, of a murder, each in their own time periods and contexts. But what is our time period and context today? How is our conception of violence changed by current technology?

Art also adopts the theme of drone fiction. Artists have long negotiated the boundary between reality and virtuality, using our common knowledge as its basic substance and transforming it into something not entirely familiar, to change our perspectives. The artist ESSAM was responsible for placing posters around New York City, purportedly advertising the New York Police Department's drone strike program—which naturally was a fiction. He adopted the actual branding of the NYPD's own PR, and used it instead to ask a question about in what ways they might use drones in the future. Will police drones mimic the military technology that preceded them? What sort of debate would there be over police drones in New York City, and whose voices would be heard? It is perhaps a sign of the poignancy of ESSAM's work that although the NYPD has expressed interest in obtaining drones, they refuse to release any information about their activities—also, that they sent counterterrorism officers after ESSAM, arresting and charging him with over fifty-six counts for various transgressions.[2]

The artist James Bridle has completed several drone-related projects, including *Drone Shadow*, the silhouette of a large military drone painted on the sidewalk in various locations, and *Dronestagram*, a social media account that posts a picture of the location of every known military drone strike and the details of what occurred. His drone work is very much about the imagery of the drone, a technology itself very much about imagery. In researching the "canonical" image of a drone—a Reaper drone firing a missile that is consistently the first result for "drone" when doing a Google Image search—he discovered something interesting. The image, used countless times as a stock photo for news media articles, is actually a computer rendering, and not a real image at all.[3] As Bridle wrote in an essay on the subject, ". . . the Canon Drone is emblematic of the liminal, self-obfuscating essence of the UAV, and all of our noumenal infrastructures. The most widely reproduced image of this most illegible of our contemporary technologies is itself a dream." It is close

FIGURE 16 Canonical drone. This 3D-rendered image of a drone has been replicated in many articles online as if it were real, becoming one of the top Google Image search results for "drone." Image by Mike Hahn.

to a drone, so much like a drone that it could fool us into thinking that it is a drone, and yet it is not, and we couldn't tell the difference.

Drone art and fiction tends to work in this unknown area, the speculative liminal space between our individual understanding of the current technology and our less conscious hopes and fears about what it could become. More interesting narrative prototyping occurs here than in "distant future" speculation. But the question remains: what do we do with this narrative? How do we use these expressions so they can affect the actual technology, and not just our social discourse?

10 OUR SELVES AND THE DRONE

What is the reason for all our narratives of the drone, and all our narratives of technology? Quite simply, narratives of technology have become a means for understanding ourselves in a world filled with technology. Our technological narratives are not just about the long path of history into contemporary times. Our technological narratives have become our history, our present, and our future. For better or for worse, we understand ourselves best with, through, and surrounded by our many technologies. And the drone, as an apparently pivotal technological narrative of our present, could be instrumental in how we think about ourselves in the coming century. We will not just have narratives about the drone. In our narratives, we will *become* the drone.

Material world

Since at least the days of Ancient Greece, we have speculated, studied, philosophized, and analyzed our relationship to the things that we make. This is a very important aspect of human existence. There are certain things we produce, like trash and other waste, which we discard without a second thought. And there are certain physical things, like art and places where we live, that we treasure forever, as if there was no more important substance in our lives. What accounts for the difference?

It is not just the materialist element of our characters that causes us to care about our objects as much as we care about ourselves. We interact with the world by changing it, by consuming some of it, reserving other parts of it, moving it around and reshaping it, transforming pieces of it and adding ourselves and our labors to it. This interaction comprises a great deal of how we understand the world and see ourselves within it.

History is itself a story about the things that we have made and destroyed, as much as it is a story of any particular people who have lived. We can trace our human ancestors with a little effort, but that only goes so far. The artifacts of our material circumstances are much easier to examine and follow throughout time. When we look at a Clovis tool—a chipped-flint cutting implement from the Paleolithic era— we can sense the way it might have been used, by imagining ourselves holding it in our hand. When we look at the Antikythera mechanism—an ancient calendar or astrolabe, the exact function of which experts still disagree upon— we feel the same sort of wonder that we do from seeing a new piece of technology and imagining what it does. It is something that we have an immediate sense for how it might be used, but we have not yet explored its exact functions and interfaces with our own hands. We feel the necessity of knowing it implicitly, just as we might know the faces and movements of our friends and loved ones, or the feel of our particular computer keyboard.

Human components

Humans, in how they relate to technology, are analogous to drones in many ways. Our images of ourselves are *bricolages*. We construct our lives out of a variety of meaningful components, adding them and taking them out as they evolve and serve the system of our lives better or worse. When cars entered human life, their speed and mobility was attached directly to our lives and livelihoods as humans themselves became capable of many things that they could not have done were they not behind the wheel of a car. That ability became augmented even further with aircraft as we made the world a smaller place, even as we threatened to blow it up with military weapons in order to justify building passenger jets. We designed computers to solve these sorts of large scale, economic problems, and then miniaturized that technology in order to fit it into our everyday lives. With robots, we took a fantasy that had been in our imaginations for centuries and adapted it to the real world, to improve things where we could with automation. Whether it is the product of the Model T or the IBM PC, the adaption of production processes in the Springfield Armory, the Ford factory, or the projectizing of the military-industrial complex, we are always improving, refining, and adapting our lives via technology.

And we also fear those changes to ourselves. Vigilante groups are forming against drones, just as they once did against cars and aircraft. A town in Colorado has proposed a hunting bounty on drones, arming themselves with shotguns just as townspeople did against cars over a hundred years ago.[1] We are thrilled about the potential of the drone to change our lives, but we are also suspicious of something that is not us having human attributes, just as we were about computers and robots. We have the desire to change our lives significantly, but we know there are consequences to such adaptation.

We augment ourselves with technology in many more ways than we might intend, and while the most hysterical potential consequences are often wrong, there are others we cannot foresee. Cars changed the shape of our cities by causing large infrastructural, safety, and environmental problems, not by frightening draft animals. Military technology is a violent and wasteful way to go about advancing technology for peaceful purposes. Computers are in everything, but that means e-waste will soon be everywhere. And when you save a life by taking a pilot out of a dangerous machine, you still end a life by firing a missile from that plane.

As crucial to human existence as technology is, we are still deeply confused and conflicted about it. All of human history is paved in our confusion, misunderstanding, and the pain that results. And yet we keep plodding ahead, because we have no other choice. Like drones, we take to the sky, deploying our new technological payloads whether we truly know how to use them or don't. We cannot choose to stop existing in history any more than we can stop drones from being part of that history. But where we do have a choice is in our ability to make a better effort at understanding that process by improving narrative systems—to orient ourselves better, to improve our command and control of the technological components in our systems, to refine our ability to sense and avoid ethical dilemmas that could prove fatal, if not to ourselves, than to the people who pass underneath our shadow.

From analogy to data

Our relationship with drones is not simply that of analogy. We know the world like drones do, because in contemporary times we must use drone technology to know a world made from data. I have described this relationship elsewhere as drone ethnography—it is the process of studying our selves and our uses of technology *with* technology.[2]

Drones are a means of data collection. They fly through the air, but they are only able to do so because they have sensors constantly collecting data, which is then fed back to the algorithms helping to control the aircraft for the operator.

Like any other form of data collection, they are only as good as the data that they have the means to collect. Whether the drone's sensors are accelerometers, LADAR, or cameras, the decisions made through drones, either by the operator or the automated algorithms, are only as good as the data the drone can collect. We can see the effect of this in the way cheap, reliable accelerometers were crucial to maintaining quadrotors' stable flight. Cheap, ubiquitous GPS has made drones able to navigate on their own outdoors. And drones are currently limited in their ability to fly indoors, because GPS signals are blocked inside of buildings and SLAM-capable LADAR units are too heavy and/or expensive for most applications.

Our ability to decide which technology to use and how to use it is becoming a process of automated data collection. The automobile may once have been modified and adapted by hobbyists and farmers, but now under our cars' hoods are sealed packages, only accessible through the data they report back to us. A drone hobbyist does not necessarily understand the accelerometer's interior functions, but can connect it to the autopilot, manipulating the stream of data. We do not understand the entire aerodynamic physics of a drone's flight through the air, or the content of each information packet our computer exchanges with the network—but we can choose the best software to do that for us. We use metrics, fed back to us from our devices, in order to make decisions on whether or not to continue using that technology.

When we invent airspace regulations in order to safely fly drones in the NAS, but do so based on the current abilities of drones without considering how they might evolve, we are navigating technology law with a SLAM system—only conceiving of the technological terrain as far as our sensors can see by line of sight. We are studying our own automated, technological existence, using nothing other than our own automated technological existence to collect data. Whether we take an egocentric or exocentric view of drone technology—by positioning ourselves within the historical development process or outside the historical development process—the mechanism itself is still the only thing there; we are simply using different sensors to collect the information on its process. The narratives we deploy to understand drones are malleable. We are studying a technological network, and doing so by collecting particular data, depending on what aspect of that network we wish to study.

Automobiles quickly became part of the United States' "national character." We understand that a "car culture" was created, because of the importance of this technology in changing how humans interacted with each other and with the objects in their world. Drone culture is growing in our society, not just through a preoccupation with what we should or should not do with drones, but because every day we act more like drones in the way that we use technology. Cars came to symbolize our personal success and mobility, and our ability to actively engage with the systems of the world to our own benefit. Drones might symbolize our technological interrelation with each other, as we begin trusting ever more elements of our lives to automation. Drones might be a symbol of our reliance upon thin streams of data, and the need to avail ourselves of many different metrics in order to navigate our world. A car contains the image of a single person, heading in a straight line across open road. Drones might tell the story of multiple people becoming part of a network, as swarms of people share data to make better decisions, availing themselves of the abilities of our new robotic friends, growing to like them as we become akin to them.

11 ESTHETICS OF THE DRONE

If we act like drones, we are also beginning to see like drones. Technology affects all aspects of perception, from the most pragmatic to the social to the esthetic. We must consider all the ways that drone-colored glasses affect not just our ideas, but also our senses and our other unconscious ways of perceiving the world. How else do we recognize a symbol, if not by its appearance? If there is to be a "drone culture," what will its trademarks look and feel like? What are the most notable aspects of the drone, which will come to represent the technological singularity of this network of narratives?

A specular technology

First and foremost, drones change the way that we see. As we discussed in the last chapter, drones herald a change of perspective in which we interact through technology through the data it collects, rather than the technology's physical existence. For drones, this data takes a number of forms, but the most important to a visually oriented species like human beings is ocular data.

Drones, at their current level of technology, allow us to observe large swaths of ground for an extended period of time. CCTV and satellite imagery each have their particular advantages for different surveillance and reconnaissance tasks. But drones allow a mobile platform that can remain over the ground at a distance that minimizes the target's awareness of the platform, while also allowing live retargeting of the area of focus.

This ever-present visual relationship permanently alters human perception. Drone sensor operators talk about the range of ways that staring through the drone's camera for hours on end can change a person.[1] It leads to a sort of tunnel vision, given the "soda straw" perspective of staring through a zoomed lens. Operators on station for long periods of time watch people below doing all sorts of mundane and daily tasks—driving, cooking, smoking, and even having sex— from a visual perspective that places them both within the scene and above the scene. The look of this perspective is normalized, in the blanked-out colors of the camera's high-contrast daylight imagery, and the monochrome white and black of the infrared camera at night. This observational position is punctuated by the violence of the drone missile strike, which is targeted using an infrared laser beam projected from the drone. When wearing special goggles, Marines on the ground can see the beam coming down out of the sky and call it "the light of God."[2] This vernacular terminology outlines the odd technological relationship the drone allows—that of generally passive observer, but with the extreme power that constant observation gives.

Mediated experience

It has become a trope in drone discourse to talk about drone operating as if it were a "video game."[3] It is supposed to be easy to fly a drone, a belief perhaps propagated by several facts: many drone operators were not pilots of manned aircraft before being trained to fly drones; the importance of automation to drone technology; and certain robots use common video-game controllers as their control interface. But given the difficulty of actually flying a drone (still quite a technical feat), this is really not true. However, what this myth speaks to is the mediated experience that technology provides.

We consider video games to be replications of reality that are *separate from* reality. We have come to call these "virtual" spaces that denote a difference in space, but not a difference that is completely estranged from our notions of space. As the philosopher Gilles Deleuze puts it, "The virtual is opposed not to the real but to the actual. The virtual is fully real in so far as it is virtual."[4]

There is a space that is opened up by technology—a virtual realm, which does not exist contrary to the actual world of facts so much as it connects different parts of reality, tunneling between them through an informational bridge. When military drone operators sit in front of their consoles, they control a drone flying in real space and time, but they only keep in touch with it through the data flowing to their screens, and the drone can only respond to their commands by the data they send back to it. The virtual space is connected to reality, but mediated by the separation of data. The human is not taken out of the loop by this automation—indeed, when the command-and-control signal sent by satellite is lost, the drone becomes nearly helpless and is forced to orbit in an attempt to regain the signal. If the signal is not found, there is a good chance the drone could fall out of the sky. If a missile has been fired when the signal is lost, it could easily miss its target and hit something entirely different. The distance between the operator and the missile is a virtual space, existing and maintained entirely by technology networks. In the same way that the virtual world of a video game can dissolve in a second with the failure of a broadband or electrical network, the effect that drones have in the world can be lost just as quickly.

And as much as the technology affects virtual space, virtual space can affect the technology. Different constructions of virtual space better enable the human operator to retain control of the drone. For example, nearly all drones are flown by operators either working from an egocentric or exocentric viewpoint. The operator is provided with either a video feed from the drone, looking outward (egocentric), or with a video feed on the ground, showing the drone (exocentric). Detailed studies have been conducted to determine the best viewpoint, and they have discovered that it varies depending on the situation.[5] In some cases a combination of ego and exocentric viewpoints are best. For the Global Hawk, a vehicle controlled with egocentric cameras, it was discovered that pilots had a great deal of confusion with the attitude indicator. An attitude indicator in a piloted aircraft typically shows a static image of the aircraft, with a rotating ball behind it representing the earth's horizon, moving around to indicate the pitch and roll of the aircraft. However, rather than this "inside-out" display, Global Hawk operators faired far better with an "outside-in" display, where the horizon stays level but the image of the aircraft moves.[6] This is a seemingly exocentric attitude indicator, paired with an egocentric camera view.

In a technological realm where the transmission of data through virtual spaces matters so much for the successful use of the technology, these sorts of representational features are only just being explored. Different automation strategies are being paired with different sorts of displays and interfaces to experiment and see what works best. Video controllers are often chosen because video game companies have many years of research on computer-human interaction that drone companies do not. Even the cell phone is being explored as a drone controller interface, to see what the vast domain of app-oriented interfaces can add to the equation.[7]

FIGURE 17 Global Hawk interface. The attitude indicator is visible, which shows the attitude of the aircraft relative to the ground—the exocentric view—rather than the attitude of the ground relative to the aircraft. Image produced by the FAA in Kevin W. Williams's *An Assessment of Pilot Control Interfaces for Unmanned Aircraft*, and is in the public domain.

Other sensory input

Drones are highly visual, but certainly not solely visual. Studies have shown that drone operators are better served with a range of sensory input, and not just visual data from cameras. Pilots benefit from what is called "multi-modal reinforcement," in which the ability to pick up on a particular sensory cue is increased if it is accompanied by another sense stimulus, like noise helping an individual to sense the difference in small light variations.[8] This multimodal reinforcement would be useful for flying the drone, for sense-and-avoid and other safety needs, but also in analyzing the sensor readout as part of the drone's primary functions. Most attempts to implement this in drone interfaces thus far take the form of simulating multimodal sensory data. In other words, additional indicators, the replication of sense data such as sound around the operator's head (vestibular input), and haptic feedback for certain conditions, all help the operator.[9] However, this is not the same as actually experiencing the sensory input. The operator is still reliant upon the drone's sensors and interface to present the information in a way that the operator can perceive.

Drones create unique sensory experiences for the people around them as well, not just for the operators. Military drones largely remain out of sight from the population below them, but they can be heard. Pashtun tribespeople in Pakistan refer to the drones overhead as "wasps" or "mosquitoes" due to their sound.[10] This sound has a psychological effect on the people who hear it for days on end. Said an unidentified man from the region quoted in an *Atlantic* article, "When children hear the drones, they get really scared, and they can hear them all the time so they're always fearful that the drone is going to attack them. … Because of the noise, we're psychologically disturbed, women, men, and children. … Twenty-four hours, a person is in stress and there is pain in his head."[11] As drones continue to deploy, we can foresee an even more complicated range of sensory inputs beginning to affect both operators and those whom drones are operated over.

The semiotics of the drone

The look and behavior of drones creates an indelible image in the minds of anyone—whether a person who flies them, a person overflown by them, or a person who sees them in media images. The bumped head of the Predator and Reaper's radome creates an anthropomorphic figure—the first go-to image that comes to mind when drones are referenced, like the false simulacra of the canonical drone discovered by James Bridle. The image of the multirotor drone is also gaining its own currency. While a small drone might look indistinguishable from any small remote-controlled aircraft, the quadrotor is most conspicuously a drone, its lack of typical airframe silhouette punctuated by the camera, most often hanging below it like a single eye. Both the Predator and the quadrotor appear to us in a very specific, drone-like way, emphasizing the ways in which this technology differs from other aircraft that have preceded it, even as they differ from each other.

The ability to kill remotely, while hardly new to military technology, finds its symbol in the shape of the drone. Post-traumatic stress disorder can affect people from any number of technological sources, and yet the cases that have accompanied military drone campaigns are linked to that image and are taken as a separate case, to be argued against or justified separately from the other horrors of war. "Drone strikes," a unique phrase considered separately from any other air strike, reinforces the notion that this is something different, with a different experiential mechanism. Paranoia about the capabilities and proliferating quantities of drones are invested into this image as well. Protesters against drone usage by the military and law enforcement organizations find a special heinousness in use of the drone, even though the same killing technology is deployed by many other means. For activist marches, rallies, and protests, special models of drones are made and carried along in marches and rallies like effigies. In the United States, a contemporary anti-war protest will almost always have a drone effigy in tow, like a totem, representing the example *par excellence* of the current state of military technology. The bumped radome appears as a skull, carried like a talisman to ward off death.

FIGURE 18 Drone effigy. Protesters' drone effigy, seen outside of teach-in at Drones and Aerial Robotics Conference in New York City, October 11, 2013. Image by the author.

What's in a name?

The military and commercial drone companies shy away from the word "drone," preferring any number of acronyms without the heavy narrative that the drone has: Unmanned Aerial System (UAS), Unmanned Vehicle (UV), Remotely Piloted Vehicle (RPV), and other alphabet-soup designations so common in the military-industrial complex. But the word "drone" was originally the military's choice, stemming back to the radio-controlled target drones built before World War Two. A drone is literally a male bee, stingless, with large eyes, good only for fertilizing the eggs of the queen. Other insect names have been applied to aerial robots by the military as well, such as Firebee, Firefly, Firebug, and Lightning Bug. There is perhaps something both dehumanizing in this term—noting the lack of pilot and its tendency to act according to a basic programming—but also something animalistic, that gives the aircraft its own sense of volition outside of the immediate control of human beings.

Despite the attempts of the military to rebrand the drone as simply another technological system, the name "drone" has stuck. This singular name works for society at large. Even though it lumps together a wide range of technologies that often have little in common across their range of applications and configurations, we seem to want a single word to define all of these technologies and to express what they mean to us. Drones have become a singular inflection point of fear, of paranoia, of wonder, of technological wizardry, and of future possibility. No other word would suffice, at this point in history, to refer to this web of concepts, meanings, and esthetics so easily. The drone might be a mythical creature, not unlike a unicorn or a zombie—not so representative of any one thing in reality, but of a virtual confluence, a place where the meaning of various technologies can join together and be grasped by our imagination before dissolving back into its component pieces again.

The more unique aspects of the drone we discover, the more apparent the drone's unique esthetic effect becomes. The esthetic of the drone is unconscious, happening on the level of sensory perception, of associative memory, and of language. But this effect is as malleable as the drone narrative; stories change over time, and so do their look and feel. A new technological advance might come along that changes drone technology as well as their esthetic effect upon us, giving drones an entirely new characteristic in our minds. A new, unforeseen, and ubiquitous use for drones might give them a new name, a new image. But until those changes occur, the current drone esthetic will continue to have a fundamental influence on our drone narrative.

12 THE DRONE AS MEME

A meme is not unlike a gene, but for ideas, behaviors, or other cultural material. The term was coined by Richard Dawkins to theorize how evolutionary principles could work on a social level. In the same way that the traits that genes express serve to propagate the gene through sexual selection, the effects of memes cause their repetition as they are shared and copied by others.

This doesn't mean that all memes are positive. A harmful meme could just as easily be spread as a beneficial meme, if it has the ability to repeat itself. The means of repetition lies in finding a niche. How catchy is a song? How well is a story told and retold? How easy is a small skill or habit to learn? How tiresome is a particular activity?

Our narratives, as much as they are constituted by facts, are largely about these mimetic devices. A narrative can mutate with the introduction of a meme to its material, if there is means for that meme to repeat and grow. And even though it is accepted that "the winners write the history books," smaller, minor stories can continue alongside the more traditional narratives of the victor, if there is the means for them to repeat themselves and live on.

What will be repeated as common truth tomorrow depends on the mechanisms of repetition that are in place today. Consider any meme of the future—flying cars for example. In the middle of the twentieth century, with the memes of the car and the aircraft finding easy means of repetition through the way they were changing everyday life, it is no surprise that these memes would find a fusion. Flying cars were practically guaranteed for the future, because the strength of cars' technology and the strength of aircraft technology would combine as easily as one and one make two. But this was not the case. The way that cars transformed transportation was completely different than the way that aircraft changed transportation. These technologies had different means of repetition, and proliferated entirely differently. We ended up with an auto industry that was financially successful (at least for half a century) because of consumer credit and buying power, and an aircraft industry that was tied directly to the military power of the American state. And yet the flying car meme continued sailing through the clouds, empty, devoid of any technological underpinning based on fact and historical content. It continued as a fantasy of science fiction, and then as part of American nostalgia for a Golden Age of science fiction, which was itself a fantasy of post-war American cultural power. As transportation ground down in oil crises, traffic jams, and freeway protests, as the auto industry departed the United States to other continents,

FIGURE 19 Avrocar. An experimental aircraft built by the US military. The craft was very unstable, and the project was eventually abandoned. Photo produced by the Department of Defense, and is in the public domain, sourced from Wikipedia.

and as the military might of American air power could not bring it back, society was left confused and disoriented, with narratives and memes that did not seem as useful as they had been decades before.

This is not a historical thesis about why things ended up the way that they did—this is about a *lack* of historical theses. It is mere speculation to wonder whether, if Americans had been more in touch with why they all suddenly had cars and not personal aircraft, we would have arrived at a different present than we did. We can no more assume that things would end up causally different than we can change the facts. The conditions were what they were, and this is the course of history.

But where speculation has value is in looking toward the future through the lens of the present. The memes of the future are not fixed. What causes them to repeat and substantiate themselves is a changing field. Unlike history, the present can be altered. We can't change the flying car meme of the twentieth century, but we can change the flying car meme of the twenty-first century.

What is the flying car of contemporary times? It may well be the drone. We don't know whether, from the perspective of the future looking back at our present, the drone will look like a flying car, any more than a computer will look like a Model T, or a drone will look like an IBM PC, or an atomic bomb, or any other analogy. All we can do is understand the narrative of the drone as best we can and respond according-ly. Our job is not to swat down memes of the drone with pes-simism any more than it is to bolster them with optimism. Our task with the narrative of the drone is to understand why the meme is so powerful, and to understand what that means for the technology.

Drones, as a technological meme, are one of the most powerful in the world today. They embody fear, paranoia, dreams, and cutting-edge technology as much or more than any other current symbol. They combine technology that is over 100 years old, with technology that is only now reaching the market. They are changing shape from day to day. Their potential uses comprise a huge, unknown terrain. Their current military use is a serious, deadly terrain. We don't know what drones will look like two years from today. As much information we have about the technology of the drone, there are as many questions waiting to be answered. As technological advances pan out or don't, as the FAA makes new rules and lawsuits are brought against them, as the military continues to attack foreign countries with drones, and as activists march in protest, we can only see a narrative that is fundamentally unpredictable.

We might not be able to completely rewrite drone memes, but we can supplement them and improve the overall narrative. Most narratives of this technology only touch on a few superficial facets. They are as thin as a protest sign, and as shallow as a corporate television commercial. But there is a wealth of content below the surface, just waiting to be incorporated into the discourse.

The technological components of drone systems are fascinating stories in and of themselves. Any advances in battery technology, electric motors, radio antennas, or algorithmic learning could change the shape of the drone meme in ways that we can only begin to imagine. The composite system that is the drone is a story that is a network of stories, any of which might do a lot of good, amplified in the meme of the drone.

We can add historical narratives to the drone meme in ways that are more complex than simply plugging in an analogy. There may not be a Model T of drones, but how would mass production change drones? Is there a commercial market that could stimulate such mass production? Or are drones going to remain like aircraft, only developed and produced insofar as they are subsidized by military use? What would engineering a standardization of drone components do? Is there a company like IBM, with a sales force and market control so powerful that if they developed a standardized "Drone PC" it would be accepted by consumers and competing manufacturers? Is a common drone operating system possible, or is the architecture of the various airframes, sensors, and power systems too complex? How well do the lessons of industrial robots apply to drones? Are they linked only through the fantasy of robot companions, or does the technological ability to fulfill certain limited needs for consistent automated precision mean that a drone is more like a welding robot than a fighter plane? Speculative answers to any of these detailed questions could be narrative-altering memes.

Many of the intentions we've used to justify and develop the technology of the drone are misguided, and with a little critical thinking could be much better. We must understand that wanting drones to be able to do tasks as diverse as delivering packages, conducting humanitarian missions, and aiding journalism doesn't mean that they can. It doesn't mean that they cannot, but the fact is that there are many technological problems (at least eleven major categories of problem, as we have found). We must understand that drones are still overwhelmingly weapons, and that any drone built today will look and serve fundamentally as a weapon, regardless of what branding we simultaneously launch. We cannot, by designing a drone with good intentions, avoid the potential privacy and safety problems that come along with that technology.

When one utilizes the power of drone technology, either as aircraft or as meme, one also assumes the responsibility to use it in an ethical way. It may serve one's business purposes to tell only half the story, but the ethical component of design requires that we strive toward completeness, accounting for the entire realm of possibility, not just barnstorm into the future. Drone memes are very potent because of the power that this technology has materially, socially, esthetically, and culturally. The drone narrative is an indicator, a blinking light of possible technological progress for a reason—drones show how a variety of technologies can come together and combine in layered, amplified effect. But by only allowing certain parts of this meme to repeat themselves we do a disservice to the technology as a whole and threaten its evolution and longevity. We see only the history we want to see, and thereby introduce flaws into its structure. Throwing technology into the sky or into the market and assuming innovation will tackle any dangers that develop is like adding speed to a drone's power source without increasing the range of its sense-and-avoid system. Or contrarily, focusing on the potential negative effect of one possible use of technology without considering the inevitability of the system as a whole is like blasting at any strange device in the sky with a gun, without wondering where the aircraft will fall when you hit it or where your bullets will go if you don't. We put people at risk in both situations, because as with any technology, the ultimate judgment of its efficacy is not how many units it sells, the viral-ness of its meme, how many targets it takes out, but how it creates lasting effect in society.

Today drones largely only kill people or spy on them. This is what they are designed to do. There could be a future in which they largely help people and are designed primarily for that purpose. However, we won't get from here to there by fantasizing it, by creating a pretty meme, or by selling half a narrative. We must get there by ethical development of the technology, and by preparing a narrative suited for that task. The meme—and the drone—must be designed better. And there is no one who can take on that task but us.

We must write a new story of the drone that is not like those we've used in the past. The fantasy of the robot has always been two-faced. On one side is the all-powerful companion, a tool that helps us to achieve new heights as a species through the successful utilization of our ingenuity. On the other side is the monster that we have created out of hubris, out of lack of understanding and foresight, which gets out of our control and causes us to suffer through the mediated technology attached to our clumsy hands. Drones will end up being neither of these robots. Two-faced robots are part of a different technological meme, an understanding of the history of technology in terms of progress or regression only. What drones will end up becoming is dependent upon how the drone meme changes, and it will necessarily differ from the memes that came before it as the technology on which it is based collides and separates in a chaotic swarm. This could be the technology that writes a new story, as it takes a new place in our world.

We have one small kernel of a drone narrative that might dig itself a niche. We have some history, some current data, and an understanding of the means by which that data was created and how it can be fed back into the system. Where that narrative goes from here is not any one person or group's responsibility. It is the responsibility of all of us.

LIST OF IMAGES

Figure 1 Daimler Reitwagen. More motorcycle than car, the 1885 Daimler Reitwagen was the first vehicle to use Daimler's internal combustion engine. Image in the public domain, sourced from Wikipedia.

Figure 2 UNIVAC on CBS. Presper Eckert and programmer Harold Sweeney show off the UNIVAC to Walter Cronkite, during the computer's 1952 appearance on CBS to correctly predict the presidential election. Image produced by the US Census Bureau, in the public domain, sourced from Haverford University.

Figure 3 Welding robots. These contemporary welding robots were manufactured by KUKA, and are working in a German BMW factory. This image is by BMW Werk Lepzig, and is licensed Creative Commons, sourced through Wikimedia Commons.

Figure 4 Two Firebees in launching position on a DC-130. These BQM-34S target drones were the precursors to the Lightning Bug, and were launched in the same manner. Department of Defense photo, in the public domain, sourced from Wikipedia.

Figure 5 MQ-1 Predator. Predator is shown here on a Naval training mission in 1995, flying over the aircraft carrier USS *Carl Vinson*. Department of Defense photo by Petty Officer 3rd Class

Jeffrey S. Viano, US Navy, in the public domain, sourced from the Department of Defense.

Figure 6 Parrot.AR drone. One of the most common and affordable hobbyist quadrotors available. Photo by Nicolas Halftermeyer, licensed Creative Commons, sourced from Wikipedia.

Figure 7 FAA airspace classification diagram. Image from *Unmanned Systems Roadmap 2007–2032*, produced by the Department of Defense, in the public domain.

Figure 8 Ford magneto assembly line. Seen in 1913, this was the first Ford assembly line, and the first in the world, allowing the Model T to be manufactured on unprecedented scales. Photo is in the public domain, sourced from Wikipedia.

Figure 9 Tethered Aerostat Radar System (TARS). This aerostat is used by the US Customs and Border Patrol, and is equipped with radar that can see ground traffic. Photo is by the US Customs and Border Patrol, and is in the public domain.

Figure 10 MiniHawk 2i Automatic License Plate Recognition System. Almost so small as to be unnoticeable, this camera system photographs license plates and instantly compares them against a police database. Photo is in the public domain, sourced from Wikipedia.

Figure 11 F-16C launching AGM-154 Joint Standoff Weapon. The AGM-154 is one of several delivery methods developed for the BLU-108. This guided glide bomb is dropped by piloted aircraft, and can glide as many as 130 kilometers to its target. Photo is by Michael Ammons of the US Air Force, and is in the public domain, sourced from Wikipedia.

Figure 12 Navy personnel and PackBot. This sailor is an explosive ordinance disposal technician, posing here with his PackBot. Photo is produced by the US Navy, and is in the public domain, sourced from Wikipedia.

Figure 13 Ikhana MQ-9. NASA purchased a MQ-9, known as the Reaper in its military variant but named Ikhana in this case, used in the Suborbital Science Program. Photo is produced by NASA, and is in the public domain, sourced from Wikipedia.

Figure 14 Matternet drone. The rendered mockup of the as yet undeveloped drone shows it flying over the wretched huts of—somewhere. Photo reproduced courtesy of Matternet.

Figure 15 1939 *R.U.R.* WPA poster. This poster was designed by the Works Progress Administration, for a production of *R.U.R.* This image was produced by the Federal Government, and is in the public domain, sourced from Wikipedia.

Figure 16 Canonical drone. This 3D-rendered image of a drone has been replicated in many articles online as if it were real, becoming one of the top Google Image search results for "drone." Image by Mike Hahn.

Figure 17 Global Hawk interface. The attitude indicator is visible, which shows the attitude of the aircraft relative to the ground—the exocentric view—rather than the attitude of the ground relative to the aircraft. Image produced by the FAA in Kevin W. Williams's *An Assessment of Pilot Control Interfaces for Unmanned Aircraft*, and is in the public domain.

Figure 18 Drone effigy. Protesters' drone effigy, seen outside of teach-in at Drones and Aerial Robotics Conference in New York City, October 11, 2013. Image by the author.

Figure 19 Avrocar. An experimental aircraft built by the US military. The craft was very unstable, and the project was eventually abandoned. Photo produced by the Department of Defense, and is in the public domain, sourced from Wikipedia.

NOTES

Chapter 1

1 James J. Flink, *The Automobile Age* (Cambridge, MA: MIT Press, 1988), 5, 33.

2 Flink, *The Automobile Age*, 17.

3 Flink, *The Automobile Age*, 52.

4 Flink, *The Automobile Age*, 54.

5 David L. Lewis and Laurence Goldstein, *The Automobile and American Culture* (Ann Arbor: University of Michigan Press, 1983), 6.

6 Michael L. Berger, *The Automobile in American History and Culture* (Westport, CN: Greenwood Press, 2001), XVII.

7 Flink, *The Automobile Age*, 151; *Automobile*, April 22, 1909, 676.

8 Flink, *The Automobile Age*, 132.

9 Peter L. Jakab, *Visions of a Flying Machine* (Washington, DC: Smithsonian Institution Press, 1990), 124–6.

10 Wilbur D. Jones, *Arming the Eagle: A History of U.S. Weapons Acquisition Since 1775* (Fort Belvoir, VA: Defense Systems Management College Press, 1999), 191.

11 Jakab, *Visions of a Flying Machine*, 218.

12 Jacob A. Vander Meulen, *The Politics of Aircraft: Building An American Military Industry* (Lawrence, KS: University Press of Kansas, 1991), 19.

13 Jones, *Arming the Eagle: A History of U.S. Weapons Acquisition Since 1775*, 199.

14 Jones, *Arming the Eagle: A History of U.S. Weapons Acquisition Since 1775*, 207.

15 Donald M. Pattillo, *A History in the Making: 80 Turbulent Years in the American General Aviation Industry* (New York: McGraw-Hill, 1998), 14.

16 Jones, *Arming the Eagle: A History of U.S. Weapons Acquisition Since 1775*, 361.

17 Vander Meulen, *The Politics of Aircraft: Building An American Military Industry*, 84.

18 Vander Meulen, *The Politics of Aircraft: Building An American Military Industry*, 92, 133.

19 War Department, *Will There Be An Aircraft in Every Garage?* (Washington, DC: War Department, 1945).

20 Mike Hally, *Electronic Brains: Stories From the Dawn of the Computer Age* (Washington, DC: Joseph Henry Press, 2005), XVII.

21 Hally, *Electronic Brains: Stories From the Dawn of the Computer Age*, 13.

22 Hally, *Electronic Brains: Stories From the Dawn of the Computer Age*, 148.

23 Michael S. Mahoney, *Histories of Computing* (Cambridge, MA: Harvard University Press, 2011), 31–2.

24 Hally, *Electronic Brains: Stories From the Dawn of the Computer Age*, 31.

25 Hally, *Electronic Brains: Stories From the Dawn of the Computer Age*, 67.

26 Hally, *Electronic Brains: Stories From the Dawn of the Computer Age*, 120–3.

27 Anthony Gandy, *The Early Computer Industry: Limitations of Scale and Scope* (Basingstoke, UK: Palgrave Macmillan, 2012), 12.

28 Gandy, *The Early Computer Industry: Limitations of Scale and Scope*, 33.

29 Mahoney, *Histories of Computing*, 35.

30 Hally, *Electronic Brains: Stories From the Dawn of the Computer Age*, 214.

31 James Chposky, *Blue Magic: The People, Power, and Politics Behind the IBM Personal Computer* (New York: Facts on File, 1988), 5.

32 Chposky, *Blue Magic: The People, Power, and Politics Behind the IBM Personal Computer*, 36.

33 A. F. T. Winfield, *Robotics: A Very Short Introduction* (Oxford: Oxford University Press, 2012), 9.

34 John Cohen, *Human Robots in Myth and Science* (London: Allen & Unwin, 1966).

35 Winfield, *Robotics: A Very Short Introduction*, 9.

36 Winfield, *Robotics: A Very Short Introduction*, 8.

Chapter 2

1 Max Boot, *War Made New: Technology, Warfare, and the Course of History, 1500 to Today* (New York: Gotham Books, 2006), 8.

2 William Hardy McNeill, *The Pursuit of Power: Technology, Armed Force, and Society since 1000 AD* (Chicago: University of Chicago Press, 1982), 70–80.

3 McNeill, *The Pursuit of Power: Technology, Armed Force, and Society since 1000 AD*, 103–11.

4 McNeill, *The Pursuit of Power: Technology, Armed Force, and Society since 1000 AD*, 220.

5 Jones, *Arming the Eagle: A History of U.S. Weapons Acquisition Since 1775*, 19–20.

6 Jones, *Arming the Eagle: A History of U.S. Weapons Acquisition Since 1775*, 54.

7 Jones, *Arming the Eagle: A History of U.S. Weapons Acquisition Since 1775*, 62.

8 Jones, *Arming the Eagle: A History of U.S. Weapons Acquisition Since 1775*, 69.

9 Jones, *Arming the Eagle: A History of U.S. Weapons Acquisition Since 1775*, 69.

10 McNeill, *The Pursuit of Power: Technology, Armed Force, and Society since 1000 AD*, 234.

11 Boot, *War Made New: Technology, Warfare, and the Course of History, 1500 to Today*, 196.

12 McNeill, *The Pursuit of Power: Technology, Armed Force, and Society since 1000 AD*, 262, 278.

13 McNeill, *The Pursuit of Power: Technology, Armed Force, and Society since 1000 AD*, 291.

14 Vander Meulen, *The Politics of Aircraft: Building An American Military Industry*, 84–5, 111.

15 Vander Meulen, *The Politics of Aircraft: Building An American Military Industry*, 188.

16 Jones, *Arming the Eagle: A History of U.S. Weapons Acquisition Since 1775*, 311.

17 Steven Zaloga, *Unmanned Aerial Vehicles: Robotic Air Warfare, 1917–2007* (Oxford: Osprey, 2008), 6.

18 Zaloga, *Unmanned Aerial Vehicles: Robotic Air Warfare, 1917–2007*, 7; Roger Hurlburt, "Monroe An Exhibit Of The Early Days Of Marilyn Monroe—Before She Became A Legend—Brings The Star's History In Focus." *Sun Sentinel*, January 6, 1991. Accessed April 13, 2014. http://articles.sun-sentinel.com/1991-01-06/features/9101010832_1_marilyn-monroe-david-conover-early-photographs.

19 Zaloga, *Unmanned Aerial Vehicles: Robotic Air Warfare, 1917–2007*, 8–9.

20 Rudi Velthuis et al., "Timeline for V-2 Attacks, 1944-45," accessed April 14, 2014. http://www.v2rocket.com/start/deployment/timeline.html; Andrew Dunar and Stephen Waring, *The Power to Explore* (Washington, DC: NASA History Office, 1999).

21 William Wagner, *Lightning Bugs and Other Reconnaissance Drones* (Washington, DC: Armed Forces Journal, 1982), 10.

22 Wagner, *Lightning Bugs and Other Reconnaissance Drones*, 17.

23 Wagner, *Lightning Bugs and Other Reconnaissance Drones*, 23.

24 Wagner, *Lightning Bugs and Other Reconnaissance Drones*, 189.

25 Wagner, *Lightning Bugs and Other Reconnaissance Drones*, 24, 196.

26 Wagner, *Lightning Bugs and Other Reconnaissance Drones*, 182.

27 Wagner, *Lightning Bugs and Other Reconnaissance Drones*, 185.

28 Jeffrey Richelson, *The Wizards of Langley: The CIA's Directorate of Science and Technology* (Boulder, CO: Westview, 2001), 26.

29 Bill Yenne, *Attack of the Drones: A History of Unmanned Aerial Combat* (St. Paul, MN: MBI Pub. Co., 2004), 36.

30 Zaloga, *Unmanned Aerial Vehicles: Robotic Air Warfare, 1917–2007*, 22.

31 Zaloga, *Unmanned Aerial Vehicles: Robotic Air Warfare, 1917–2007*, 24–5.

32 Yenne, *Attack of the Drones: A History of Unmanned Aerial Combat*, 37.

33 Yenne, *Attack of the Drones: A History of Unmanned Aerial Combat*, 60.

34 Yenne, *Attack of the Drones: A History of Unmanned Aerial Combat*, 66.

Chapter 3

1 *Flight*, January 24, 1924. Accessed April 13, 2014. http://www. flightglobal.com/pdfarchive/view/1924/1924%20-%200047. html, 47.

2 Yuan Gao, "What Makes The Quadcopter Design So Great For Small Drones?" *Forbes*, January 23, 2013. Accessed April 13, 2014. http://www.forbes.com/sites/quora/2013/12/23/what-makes-the-quadcopter-design-so-great-for-small-drones/.

3 VeraTech website. Accessed April 13, 2014. https://web. archive.org/web/20131216122239/http://veratechcorp.com/ company.html; Jay Sloat, "Roswell Flyer Modifications." Accessed April 13, 2014. http://www.charlesriverrc.org/ articles/kitmods/jaysloat_roswellmods.htm.

4 Johann Borenstein, *The HoverBot—An Electrically Powered Flying Robot* (Ann Arbor: University of Michigan, 1992), 4.

5 Eryk Brian Nice, *Design of a Four Rotor Hovering Vehicle* (Master's Thesis, Cornell University, 2004), 14.

6 Nice, *Design of a Four Rotor Hovering Vehicle*, 14.

7 Aerospace Control Laboratories MIT, "Project News." Accessed April 14, 2014. http://vertol.mit.edu/news.html; Vlad Savov, "Autonomous quadrocopter flies through windows, straight into our hearts." Accessed April 13, 2014. http://www.engadget.com/2010/05/28/autonomous-quadrocopter-flies-through-windows-straight-into-our/.

8 Tim Fernholz, "The private drone industry is like Apple in 1984." Accessed April 13, 2014. http://qz.com/46893/the-private-drone-industry-is-like-apple-in-1984/.

9 U.S. Congress, Committee on Armed Services, *The Defense Industrial Base: The Role of the Department of Defense* (Washington, DC: U.S. Government Printing Office, 2012); U.S. Congress, Office of Technology Assessment, *Holding the Edge: Maintaining the Defense Technology Base* (Washington, DC: U.S. Government Printing Office, 1989); Government Accountability Office, *DOD Efforts to Adopt Open Systems for Its Unmanned Aircraft Systems Have Progressed Slowly* (Washington, DC: U.S. Government Printing Office, 2013).

10 Joseph N. Mait and Jon G. Grossman, "Relevancy and Risk: The U.S. Army and Future Combat Systems," (*Defense Horizons*, May 2002), 3.

11 U.S. Congress, Committee on Armed Services, *The Defense Industrial Base: The Role of the Department of Defense*, 27.

12 Jones, *Arming the Eagle: a History of U.S. Weapons Acquisition Since 1775*, 460.

13 Donald M. Pattillo, *A History in the Making: 80 Turbulent Years in the American General Aviation Industry* (New York: McGraw-Hill, 1998), 3.

14 Department of Defense, *Unmanned Systems Roadmap 2007–2032* (Washington, DC: Department of Defense, 2007), 108.

15 Department of Defense, *Unmanned Systems Roadmap 2007–2032*, 107.

16 Government Accountability Office, *Measuring Progress and Addressing Potential Privacy Concerns Would Facilitate Integration into the National Airspace System* (Washington, DC: U.S. Government Printing Office, 2012), 18.

17 Government Accountability Office, *Measuring Progress and Addressing Potential Privacy Concerns Would Facilitate Integration into the National Airspace System*, 19.

18 Government Accountability Office, *Use in the National Airspace System and the Role of the Department of Homeland Security* (Washington, DC: U.S. Government Printing Office, 2012), 8.

19 U.S. Congress, Committee on Homeland Security, *Using Unmanned Aerial Systems within the Homeland: Security Game-Changer?* (Washington, DC: U.S. Government Printing Office, 2013), 14.

20 Kevin W. Williams, *A Summary of Unmanned Aircraft Accident/Incident Data: Human Factors Implications* (Washington, DC: FAA, Office of Aerospace Medicine, 2004), 1.

Chapter 4

1 Mahoney, *Histories of Computing*, 35.

2 Patrick Lin, Keith Abney, and George A. Bekey, eds, *Robot Ethics: The Ethical and Social Implications of Robots* (Cambridge, MA: MIT Press, 2012), 3.

3 Government Accountability Office, *DOD Efforts to Adopt Open Systems for Its Unmanned Aircraft Systems Have Progressed Slowly*, 13.

4 Fernholz, "The private drone industry is like Apple in 1984."

5 Wagner, *Lightning Bugs and Other Reconnaissance Drones*, 1.

6 Mahoney, *Histories of Computing*, 35.

7 Lewis Mumford, *The Myth of the Machine* (New York: Harcourt, 1967), 188.

8 James Burke, *Connections* (New York: Simon & Schuster, 2007), 289.

9 Hally, *Electronic Brains: Stories From the Dawn of the Computer Age*, 41.

10 Flink, *The Automobile Age*, 24.

11 Lewis and Goldstein, *The Automobile and American Culture*, 6–7.

12 Flink, *The Automobile Age*, 41.

13 Flink, *The Automobile Age*, 214.

14 Flink, *The Automobile Age*, 219.

Chapter 5

1 Craig Timberg, "Blimplike surveillance craft set to deploy over Maryland heighten privacy concerns," *Washington Post*, January 22, 2014.

2 Rainer K. L. Trummer, *Design and Implementation of the Javiator Quadrotor: An Aerial Software Testbed* (PhD dissertation, University of Salzburg, 2010), 11.

3 Regina A. Pomranky, *Human Robotics Interaction Army Technology Objective Raven Small Unmanned Aerial Vehicle*

Task Analysis and Modeling (Aberdeen, MD: US Army Research Laboratory, 2006), 1.

4 Borenstein, *The HoverBot—An Electrically Powered Flying Robot*, 4.

5 Cheryl L. Klipp and Edward Measure, *Urban Turbulence and Wind Gusts for Micro Air Vehicle Bio-inspired Designs* (Adelphi, MD: Army Research Laboratory, 2011), 10–21.

6 Williams, *A Summary of Unmanned Aircraft Accident/Incident Data: Human Factors Implications*, 1.

7 Kevin W. Williams, *Human Factors Implications of Unmanned Aircraft Accidents: Flight-Control Problems* (Washington, DC: FAA, Office of Aerospace Medicine, 2006), 5.

8 Mahoney, *Histories of Computing*, 68.

9 Lin, Abney, and Bekey, eds, *Robot Ethics: The Ethical and Social Implications of Robots*, 63.

10 Kevin W. Williams, *An Assessment of Pilot Control Interfaces for Unmanned Aircraft* (Washington, DC: FAA, Office of Aerospace Medicine, 2007), 59.

Chapter 6

1 Richelson, *The Wizards of Langley: The CIA's Directorate of Science and Technology*, 198–200.

2 Jennifer Lynch and Peter Bibring, "Automated License Plate Readers Threaten Our Privacy," *Electronic Frontier Foundation*, May 6, 2013.

3 Hanni Fakhoury, "When a Secretive Stingray Cell Phone Tracking 'Warrant' Isn't a Warrant," *Electronic Frontier Foundation*, March 23, 2013.

4 Government Accountability Office, *Use in the National Airspace System and the Role of the Department of Homeland Security*; Government Accountability Office, *Measuring Progress and Addressing Potential Privacy Concerns Would Facilitate Integration into the National Airspace System*; U.S. Congress, Committee on Science, Space, and Technology, *Operating Unmanned Aircraft Systems in the National Airspace System: Assessing Research and Development Efforts to Ensure Safety* (Washington, DC: U.S. Government Printing Office, 2013).

5 Melanie Mason, "California Assembly approves limits on drones, paparazzi," *Los Angeles Times*, January 29, 2014.

6 Burkhard Bilger, "Auto Correct: Has the Self-Driving Car At Last Arrived?" *The New Yorker*, November 25, 2013.

7 Textron Systems, *BLU-108 Sub-munition.* Accessed April 13, 2014. http://www.textrondefense.com/sites/default/files/datasheets/blu108_datasheet.pdf.

8 Lin, Abney, and Bekey, eds, *Robot Ethics: The Ethical and Social Implications of Robots*, 5

9 Stuart H. Young, and Hung M. Nguyen, *Small Robot Team System Design* (Adelphi, MD: Army Research Laboratory, 2003), 15.

10 Raja Parasuraman, Thomas B. Sheridan, and Christopher D. Wickens, and "A Model for Types and Levels of Human Interaction with Automation" *IEEE Transactions on Systems, Man, and Cybernetics—Part A: Systems and Humans* 30, 3 (May 2000): 1.

11 Lin, Abney, and Bekey, eds, *Robot Ethics: The Ethical and Social Implications of Robots*, 113.

12 Wagner, *Lightning Bugs and Other Reconnaissance Drones*, 189.

Chapter 7

1 InsideDefense.com, "Global Hawk Program Manager Plans For Early Deliveries, Budget Cuts." Accessed April 13, 2014. http://insidedefense.com/index.php?option=com_user& view=login&return=aHR0cDovL2luc2lkZWRlZmVuc2 UuY29tL1VubWFubmVkLVN5c3RlbXMvV2Vla2x5LU FsZXJ0L0L3dlZWtseS1hbGVydC1qYW51YXJ5LTIyLTIw MTMvbWVudS1pcZC04OTUuaHRtbA.

2 Chris Jones, "Brewer delivers a buzz to ice fishermen via drone," *USA Today*, January 31, 2014.

3 Sean H. Breheny and Raffaello D'Andrea, "Using Airborne Vehicle-Based Antenna Arrays to Improve Communications with UAV Clusters," *Proceedings of the 42nd IEEE Conference on Decision and Control Maui*, Hawaii USA, December 2003.

4 U.S. Congress, Committee on Homeland Security, *Using Unmanned Aerial Systems within the Homeland: Security Game-Changer?*, 2.

5 U.S. Congress, Committee on Homeland Security, *Using Unmanned Aerial Systems within the Homeland: Security Game-Changer?*, 12.

Chapter 8

1 Government Accountability Office, *Measuring Progress and Addressing Potential Privacy Concerns Would Facilitate Integration into the National Airspace System*, 11.

2 U.S. Congress, Committee on Science, Space, and Technology, *Operating Unmanned Aircraft Systems in the National Airspace System: Assessing Research and Development Efforts to Ensure Safety*, 63.

3 Nidhi Subbaraman, "FAA Fine Against Drone Photographer Dismissed," *NBC News*, March 7, 2014.

4 Dana Liebelson, "Now There's a Zombie Drone That Hunts, Controls, and Kills Other Drones," *Mother Jones*, December 6, 2013.

5 "Researchers Use Spoofing to 'Hack' into a Flying Drone," *BBC*, June 29, 2012.

6 Medea Benjamin, *Drone Warfare: Killing by Remote Control* (London: Verso, 2013), ch. 1.

7 U.S. Congress, Committee on Homeland Security, *Using Unmanned Aerial Systems within the Homeland: Security Game-Changer?*, 54–5.

8 Alyssa Brown and Frank Newport, "In U.S., 65% Support Drone Attacks on Terrorists Abroad," *Gallup*, March 25, 2013.

9 Joan Lowy, "AP-NCC Poll: A Third of the Public Fears Police Use of Drones for Surveillance will Erode their Privacy," *Associated Press*, September 27, 2013.

Chapter 9

1 Cohen, *Human Robots in Myth and Science*, 105.

2 Hamilton Nolan, "NYPD Proves Street Artist Right by Tracking Him Down and Arresting Him," *Gawker*, November 30, 2012.

3 James Bridle, *One Visible Future*, March 8, 2013.

Chapter 10

1 Russell Brandom, "Colorado town proposes $100 'drone bounty'," *The Verge*, July 18, 2013; Lewis and Goldstein, *The Automobile and American Culture*, 38.

2 Adam Rothstein, "Drone Ethnography," *Rhizome*, July 20, 2011.

Chapter 11

1 Matthew Power, "Confessions of a Drone Warrior," *GQ*, October 23, 2013; Matt J. Martin, *Predator* (Minneapolis, MN: Zenith Press, 2010).

2 "Dread" *Dread Exhibition*, July 31, 2013.

3 Benjamin, *Drone Warfare: Killing by Remote Control*, ch. 4.

4 Gilles Deleuze, *Difference & Repetition* (New York: Columbia University Press, 1993), 208.

5 O. Olmos, C. D. Wickens, and A. Chudy, "Tactical Displays for Combat Awareness: An Examination of Dimensionality and Frame of Reference Concepts and the Application of Cognitive Engineering," *The International Journal of Aviation Psychology* (2000); L. C. Thomas and C. D. Wickens, "Visual Displays and Cognitive Tunneling: Frames of Reference Effects on Spatial Judgments and Change Detection," *Proceedings of Human Factors and Ergonomics Society 45th Annual Meeting* (2001), 1.

6 Williams, *An Assessment of Pilot Control Interfaces for Unmanned Aircraft*, 6.

7   Rosemarie E. Yagoda, and Susan G. Hill, *Using Mobile Devices for Robotic Controllers: Examples and Some Initial Concepts for Experimentation* (Aberdeen, MD: Army Research Laboratory, 2010).

8   Williams, *Documentation of Sensory Information in the Operation of Unmanned Aircraft Systems*, 1.

9   Williams, *Documentation of Sensory Information in the Operation of Unmanned Aircraft Systems*, 10.

10   Declan Walsh, "Obama's Enthusiasm for Drone Strikes Takes Heavy Toll on Pakistan's Tribesmen," *The Guardian*, October 7, 2010.

11   Conor Friedersdorf, "'Every Person Is Afraid of the Drones': The Strikes' Effect on Life in Pakistan," *The Atlantic*, September 25, 2012.

BIBLIOGRAPHY

Aerospace Control Laboratories at MIT. "Project News." Accessed
    April 14, 2014. http://www.vertol.mit.edu/news.html.

BBC. "Researchers use spoofing to 'hack' into a flying drone."
    June 29, 2012. Accessed April 13, 2014. http://www.bbc.com/
    news/technology-18643134.

Benjamin, Medea. *Drone Warfare: Killing by Remote Control.*
    London: Verso, 2013.

Berger, Michael L. *The Automobile in American History and
    Culture.* Westport, CN: Greenwood Press, 2001.

Bilger, Burkhard. "Auto Correct: Has the Self-Driving Car
    At Last Arrived?" *The New Yorker*, November 25, 2013.
    Accessed April 13, 2014. http://www.newyorker.com/
    reporting/2013/11/25/131125fa_fact_bilger?currentPage=all.

Boot, Max. *War Made New: Technology, Warfare, and the Course of
    History, 1500 to Today.* New York: Gotham Books, 2006.

Borenstein, Johann. *The Hoverbot—An Electrically Powered Flying
    Robot.* Draft white paper, Ann Arbor: University of Michigan,
    1992.

Brandom, Russell. "Colorado town proposes $100 'drone bounty.'"
    The Verge, July 18, 2013. Accessed April 13, 2014. http://www.
    theverge.com/2013/7/18/4535746/colorado-town-proposes-
    100-dollar-drone-bounty.

Breheny, Sean H. and Raffaelo D'Andrea. "Using Airborne Vehicle-
    Based Antenna Arrays to Improve Communications with UAV

Clusters." *Proceedings of the 42nd IEEE Conference on Decision and Control Maui*, Hawaii USA, December 2003.

Bridle, James. *One Visible Future.* March 8, 2013. Accessed April 13, 2014. http://www.onevisiblefuture.tumblr.com/post/44865882761/i-have-something-of-an-obsession-with-the-image.

Brown, Alyssa and Frank Newport. "In U.S., 65% Support Drone Attacks on Terrorists Abroad." *Gallup*, March 25, 2013. Accessed April 13, 2014. http://www.gallup.com/poll/161474/support-drone-attacks-terrorists-abroad.aspx.

Burke, James. *Connections.* New York: Simon & Schuster, 2007.

Chposky, James. *Blue Magic: The People, Power, and Politics behind the IBM Personal Computer.* New York: Facts on File, 1988.

Cohen, John. *Human Robots in Myth and Science.* London: Allen & Unwin, 1966.

Deleuze, Gilles. *Difference and Repetition.* New York: Columbia University Press, 1993.

Department of Defense. *Unmanned Systems Roadmap 2007–2032.* Washington, DC: Department of Defense, 2007.

Dread Exhibition. "Dread." July 31, 2013. Accessed April 13, 2014. http://www.thedreadexhibition.com/post/56968149235/james-bridle-london-1980-the-light-of-god.

Dunar, Andrew and Stephen Waring. *The Power to Explore.* Washington, DC: NASA History Office, 1999. Accessed April 13, 2014. http://history.msfc.nasa.gov/vonbraun/excerpts.html.

Edgerton, David. *The Shock of the Old.* Oxford: Oxford University Press, 2011.

Fakhoury, Hanni. "When a Secretive Stingray Cell Phone Tracking 'Warrant' Isn't a Warrant." *Electronic Frontier Foundation*, March 23, 2013. Accessed April 13, 2014. https://www.eff.org/deeplinks/2013/03/when-stingray-warrant-isnt-warrant.

Fernholz, Tim. "The private drone industry is like Apple in 1984." *Quartz*, January 25, 2013. Accessed April 13, 2014. http://www.qz.com/46893/the-private-drone-industry-is-like-apple-in-1984/.

Friedersdorf, Conor. "'Every Person Is Afraid of the Drones': The Strikes' Effect on Life in Pakistan." *The Atlantic*, September 25, 2012. Accessed April 13, 2014. http://www.theatlantic.com/international/archive/2012/09/every-person-is-afraid-of-the-drones-the-strikes-effect-on-life-in-pakistan/262814/.

Flight, January 24, 1924. Accessed April 13, 2014. http://www.flightglobal.com/pdfarchive/view/1924/1924%20-%200047.html.

Flink, James J. *The Automobile Age.* Cambridge, MA: MIT Press, 1988.

Gandy, Anthony. *The Early Computer Industry: Limitations of Scale and Scope.* Basingstoke, UK: Palgrave Macmillan, 2012.

Gao, Yuan. "What Makes The Quadcopter Design So Great For Small Drones?" *Forbes,* January 23, 2013. Accessed April 13, 2014. http://www.forbes.com/sites/quora/2013/12/23/what-makes-the-quadcopter-design-so-great-for-small-drones/.

Government Accountability Office. *Measuring Progress and Addressing Potential Privacy Concerns Would Facilitate Integration into the National Airspace System.* Washington, DC: US Government Printing Office, 2012.

—. *Use in the National Airspace System and the Role of the Department of Homeland Security.* Washington, DC: US Government Printing Office, 2012.

—. *DOD Efforts to Adopt Open Systems for Its Unmanned Aircraft Systems Have Progressed Slowly.* Washington, DC: US Government Printing Office, 2013.

Hally, Mike. *Electronic Brains: Stories From the Dawn of the Computer Age.* Washington, DC: Joseph Henry Press, 2005.

Hurlburt, Roger. "Monroe An Exhibit Of The Early Days Of Marilyn Monroe—Before She Became A Legend—Brings The Star's History In Focus." *Sun Sentinel,* January 6, 1991. Accessed April 13, 2014. http://articles.sun-sentinel.com/1991-01-06/features/9101010832_1_marilyn-monroe-david-conover-early-photographs.

InsideDefense.com. "Global Hawk Program Manager Plans For Early Deliveries, Budget Cuts." January 22, 2013. Accessed April 13, 2014. http://www.insidedefense.com/index. php?option=com_user&view=login&return=aHR0cDo- vL2luc2lkZWRlZmVuc2UuY29tL1VubWFubmVkLVN5c3Rlb XMvV2Vla2x5LUFsZXJ0L3dlZWtseS1hbGVydC1qYW51YXJ5 LTIyLTIwMTMvbWVudS1pZmC04OTAuaHRtbA.

Jakab, Peter L. *Visions of A Flying Machine.* Washington, DC: Smithsonian Institution Press, 1990.

Jones, Chris. "Brewer delivers a buzz to ice fishermen via drone." *USA Today,* January 31, 2014. Accessed April 13, 2014. http:// www.usatoday.com/story/tech/2014/01/31/wisconsin-beer- drone/5086215/.

Jones, Wilbur D. *Arming the Eagle: A History of U.S. Weapons Acquisition Since 1775.* Fort Belvoir, VA: Defense Systems Management College Press, 1999.

Klipp, Cheryl L. and Edward Measure. *Urban Turbulence and Wind Gusts for Micro Air Vehicle Bio-Inspired Designs.* Adelphi, MD: Army Research Laboratory, 2011.

Lewis, David L. and Laurence Goldstein (eds). *The Automobile and American Culture.* Ann Arbor: University of Michigan Press, 1983.

Liebelson, Dana. "Now There's a Zombie Drone That Hunts, Controls, and Kills Other Drones." *Mother Jones,* December 6, 2013. Accessed April 13, 2014. http://www.motherjones.com/ mojo/2013/12/zombie-drone-samy-kamkar-amazon-security.

Lin, Patrick, Keith Abney, and George A. Bekey (eds). *Robot Ethics: The Ethical and Social Implications of Robots.* Cambridge, MA: MIT Press, 2012.

Lowy, Joan. "AP-NCC Poll: A third of the public fears police use of drones for surveillance will erode their privacy." *Associated Press,* September 27, 2013. Accessed April 13, 2014. http://www. ap-gfkpoll.com/uncategorized/our-latest-poll-findings-13.

Lynch, Jennifer and Peter Bibring. "Automated License Plate Readers Threaten Our Privacy." *Electronic Frontier Foundation*, May 6, 2013. Accessed April 13, 2014. https://www.eff.org/deeplinks/2013/05/alpr.

Mahoney, Michael S. *Histories of Computing*. Cambridge, MA: Harvard University Press, 2011.

Mait, Joseph N. and Jon G. Grossman. "Relevancy and Risk: The U.S. Army and Future Combat Systems." *Defense Horizons*, May 2002.

Martin, Matt J. *Predator: The Remote-Control Air War over Iraq and Afghanistan*. Minneapolis, MN: Zenith Press, 2010.

Mason, Melanie. "California Assembly approves limits on drones, paparazzi." *Los Angeles Times*, January 29, 2014. Accessed April 13, 2014. http://www.latimes.com/local/political/la-me-pc-assembly-floor-bills-20140129,0,66786.story#axzz2rtEsHmQm.

McNeill, William Hardy. *The Pursuit of Power: Technology, Armed Force, and Society since 1000 AD*. Chicago: University of Chicago Press, 1982.

Mumford, Lewis. *The Myth of the Machine*. New York: Harcourt, 1967.

Nice, Eryk Brian. *Design of A Four Rotor Hovering Vehicle*. Master's Thesis, Cornell University, 2004.

Nolan, Hamilton. "NYPD Proves Street Artist Right by Tracking Him Down and Arresting Him." *Gawker*, November 30, 2012. Accessed April 13, 2014. http://gawker.com/5964619/nypd-proves-street-artist-right-by-tracking-him-down-and-arresting-him.

Olmos, O., C. D. Wickens, and A. Chudy. "Tactical Displays for Combat Awareness: An Examination of Dimensionality and Frame of Reference Concepts and the Application of Cognitive Engineering." *The International Journal of Aviation Psychology* 10, 3 (2000): 247–71.

Parasuraman, Raja, Thomas B. Sheridan, and Christopher D. Wickens. "A Model for Types and Levels of Human Interaction with Automation." *IEEE Transactions on Systems, Man, and Cybernetics—Part A: Systems and Humans* 30, 3 (May, 2000): 286–97.

Pattillo, Donald M. *A History in the Making: 80 Turbulent Years in the American General Aviation Industry*. New York: McGraw-Hill, 1998.

Pomranky, Regina A. *Human Robotics Interaction Army Technology Objective Raven Small Unmanned Aerial Vehicle Task Analysis and Modeling*. Aberdeen, MD: US Army Research Laboratory, 2006.

Power, Matthew. "Confessions of a Drone Warrior." *GQ*, October 23, 2013. Accessed April 13, 2014. http://www.gq.com/news-politics/big-issues/201311/drone-uav-pilot-assassination.

Richelson, Jeffery. *The Wizards of Langley: The CIA's Directorate of Science and Technology*. Boulder, CO: Westview, 2001.

Rothstein, Adam. "Drone Ethnography." *Rhizome*, July 20, 2011. Accessed April 13, 2014. http://www.rhizome.org/editorial/2011/jul/20/drone-ethnography/.

Savov, Vlad. "Autonomous quadrocopter flies through windows, straight into our hearts." *Engadget*, May 28, 2010. Accessed April 13, 2014. http://www.engadget.com/2010/05/28/autonomous-quadrocopter-flies-through-windows-straight-into-our/.

Sloat, Jay. "Roswell Flyer Modifications." April 1999. Accessed April 13, 2014. http://www.charlesriverrc.org/articles/kitmods/jaysloat_roswellmods.htm.

Subbaraman, Nidhi. "FAA Fine Against Drone Photographer Dismissed." *NBC News*, March 7, 2014. Accessed April 13, 2014. http://www.nbcnews.com/tech/innovation/faa-fine-against-drone-photographer-dismissed-n46506.

Textron Systems. *BLU-108 Submunition*. Accessed April 13, 2014. http://www.textrondefense.com/sites/default/files/datasheets/blu108_datasheet.pdf.

Thomas, L. C. and C. D. Wickens. "Visual Displays and Cognitive Tunneling: Frames of Reference Effects on Spatial Judgments and Change Detection." *Proceedings of Human Factors and Ergonomics Society 45th Annual Meeting* 45, 4 (2001): 336–40.

Timberg, Craig. "Blimplike surveillance craft set to deploy over Maryland heighten privacy concerns." *Washington Post*, January 22, 2014. Accessed April 13, 2014. http://www.washingtonpost.com/business/technology/blimplike-surveillance-crafts-set-to-deploy-over-maryland-heighten-privacy-concerns/2014/01/22/71a48796-7ca1-11e3-95c6-0a7aa80874bc_story.html.

Trummer, Rainer K. L. "Design and Implementation of the Javiator Quadrotor: An Aerial Software Test Bed." PhD diss., University of Salzburg, 2010.

U.S. Congress, Committee on Armed Services. *The Defense Industrial Base: The Role of the Department of Defense*. Hearing before the Panel on Business Challenges Within The Defense Industry, November 1, 2011. Washington, DC: U.S. Government Printing Office, 2012.

U.S. Congress, Committee on Homeland Security. *Using Unmanned Aerial Systems within the Homeland: Security Game-Changer?* Hearing before the Subcommittee on Oversight, Investigations, and Management, July 19, 2012. Washington, DC: U.S. Government Printing Office, 2013.

U.S. Congress, Committee on Science, Space, and Technology. *Operating Unmanned Aircraft Systems in the National Airspace System: Assessing Research and Development Efforts to Ensure Safety*. Hearing before the Subcommittee on Oversight, February 15, 2013. Washington, DC: U.S. Government Printing Office, 2013.

U.S. Congress, Office of Technology Assessment. *Holding the Edge: Maintaining the Defense Technology Base*. Washington, DC: U.S. Government Printing Office, 1989.

Vander Meulen, Jacob A. *The Politics of Aircraft: Building An American Military Industry*. Lawrence, KS: University Press of Kansas, 1991.

Velthuis, Rudi, et al. "Timeline for V-2 Attacks, 1944–45." Accessed April 14, 2014. http://www.v2rocket.com/start/deployment/timeline.html.

VeraTech. "VeraTech Company information page." Archived by Archive.org. Accessed April 13, 2014. https://www.web.archive.org/web/20131216122239/http://veratechcorp.com/company.html.

Wagner, William. *Lightning Bugs and Other Reconnaissance Drones*. Washington, DC: Armed Forces Journal, 1982.

Walsh, Declan. "Obama's enthusiasm for drone strikes takes heavy toll on Pakistan's tribesmen." *The Guardian,* October 7, 2010. Accessed April 13, 2014. http://www.theguardian.com/world/2010/oct/07/pakistan-drone-missile-obama-increased.

War Department. *GI Roundtable: Will There Be a Plane in Every Garage?* Washington, DC: War Department, 1945.

Williams, Kevin W. *A Summary of Unmanned Aircraft Accident/Incident Data: Human Factors Implications*. Washington, DC: FAA, Office of Aerospace Medicine, 2004.

—. *Human Factors Implications of Unmanned Aircraft Accidents: Flight-Control Problems*. Washington, DC: FAA, Office of Aerospace Medicine, 2006.

—. *An Assessment of Pilot Control Interfaces for Unmanned Aircraft*. Washington, DC: FAA, Office of Aerospace Medicine, 2007.

—. *Documentation of Sensory Information in the Operation of Unmanned Aircraft Systems*. Washington, DC: FAA, Office of Aerospace Medicine, 2008.

Winfield, A. F. T. *Robotics: A Very Short Introduction*. Oxford: Oxford University Press, 2012.

Yagoda, Rosemarie E. and Susan G. Hill. *Using Mobile Devices for Robotic Controllers: Examples and Some Initial Concepts for Experimentation*. Aberdeen, MD: Army Research Laboratory, 2010.

Yenne, Bill. *Attack of the Drones: A History of Unmanned Aerial Combat*. St. Paul, MN: MBI Pub. Co., 2004.

Young, Stuart H. and Hung M. Nguyen. *Small Robot Team System Design*. Adelphi, MD: Army Research Laboratory, 2003.

Zaloga, Steven. *Unmanned Aerial Vehicles: Robotic Air Warfare, 1917–2007*. Oxford: Osprey, 2008.

INDEX

Note: Page references for illustrations appear in *italics*.